Treating Posttraumatic Stress Disorder Using Cognitive Behavioral Therapy Skills and Interventions

Books in This Series

Crisis Intervention for Community Behavioral Health Service Providers in Ohio

Overcoming Reluctance in Therapeutic Relationships

Psychotherapy for Families

Therapeutic Behavioral Services Using Interventions Based on Principles and Techniques of Cognitive Behavioral Therapy

Treating Attention Deficit Hyperactivity Disorder, Impulsivity, and Disruptive Behaviors in Children Using Behavioral Skill Building and Cognitive Behavioral Therapy Skills and Interventions

Treating Anxiety Using Cognitive Behavioral Therapy Skills and Interventions

Treating Depression Using Cognitive Behavioral Therapy Skills and Interventions

Treating Posttraumatic Stress Disorder Using Cognitive Behavioral Therapy Skills and Interventions

Treating Posttraumatic Stress Disorder Using Cognitive Behavioral Therapy Skills and Interventions

TREATMENT AND INTERVENTION MANUAL

Reinhild Boehme, LISW-S

Benjamin Kearney, PhD, *series editor*

THE INSTITUTE OF
FAMILY & COMMUNITY IMPACT

An OhioGuidestone Company
Berea, Ohio

Nothing contained in the manual is, or should be considered or used as, a sub-stitute for medical advice, diagnosis, or treatment. The manual is not intended to replace, and does not replace, the specialized training and professional judgment of a health care or mental health care professional. Individuals should seek the advice of a physician or other health care provider with any questions regard-ing medications, personal health or medical conditions. This manual has been prepared as a tool to assist providers. In its efforts to provide information that is accurate and generally in accord with the standards of practice at the time of publication, the author has checked with sources believed to be reliable. However, in view of the possibility of human error or changes in behavioral, mental health, or medical sciences, neither the author, nor the editor and publisher, nor any other party who has been involved in the preparation or publication of this work warrants that the information contained herein is in every respect accurate or complete, and they are not responsible for any errors or omissions, or the results obtained from the use of such information. Further, the information presented in this manual does not constitute legal or financial advice or opinions. The ultimate responsibility for correct billing lies with the provider of the services. The reader should consult the current version of the relevant laws, regulations, and rulings.

The Institute of Family and Community Impact
An OhioGuidestone Company
www.OhioGuidestone.org

ISBN 978-1-7328190-9-2
Printed in the United States of America

In memory of my brother Volker, who walked before me with courage and grace.
You opened my eyes to beauty and wonder.

Contents

Preface

For mental health professionals, building trusting relationships with clients and knowing which interventions will most benefit them are challenging enough. Helping clients who are also dealing at the same time with chronic conditions such as poverty, violence, and addiction can seem overwhelming. That's especially true for behavioral health service providers who have limited experience. That's why we at OhioGuidestone have developed this series of clinical manuals to help professionals develop their skills while providing effective treatment.

OhioGuidestone, the largest community behavioral health organization in Ohio, regularly trains new therapists and other behavioral health interventionists to work with clients who face severe, therapy-interfering challenges. We've brought that experience to these manuals.

In this era of managed care oversight, tight funding, and pressure to deliver evidence-based or informed care, it is essential for new therapists to get up to speed on best practices quickly. It is also essential for experienced clinicians to be well provided with effective and varied treatment plans. The manuals in this series provide step-by-step guidance on evidence-based and informed treatment modalities and interventions that can be used by both licensed and unlicensed mental health professionals—as well as by their supervisors for training purposes.

Seasoned mental health professionals will find the resources offered in these manuals useful for developing a renewed focus on evidence- and research-based interventions. At OhioGuidestone, our interventions are grounded in cognitive behavioral science and also shaped by the relational and attachment scientific advances that continue to inform the behavioral health field (especially the interpersonal neurobiology work published by W. W. Norton & Company). We understand the demands of serving client populations experiencing trauma and toxic stress. Our interventions are designed not to address discrete diagnoses (clients often have more than one) but rather the symptoms that are related to them. The series addresses a wide range of issues, such as depression, anxiety, ADHD, PTSD, and even reluctance to engage in therapy, and it provides interventions for children and adults.

We cannot "fix" our clients. But we can guide them along clear paths toward developing the skills they need to navigate the challenges they face, in their thoughts and in their lives. It's our sincere hope that the books in this series will help better prepare more mental health professionals to do just that.

— Benjamin Kearney, PhD, series editor

If you purchased this manual and want to make copies of interventions to help your clients, please do so. However, please do not share copies with other professionals but encourage them to buy manuals for themselves. This will help us continue to add to and update this series, to better equip all helpers who make a difference.

Introduction

This manual is for licensed mental health providers who provide psychotherapy and related services.

Treating clients suffering from posttraumatic stress disorder and related disorders can be challenging, even for a seasoned practitioner. This is partially due to the fact that posttraumatic stress disorder is *about something*. The reasons for your client's distress are known. Your client has experienced trauma, and the symptoms are an expression of, and the result of, the traumatic experience.

When a client presents with symptoms of posttraumatic stress, there is always a difficult story waiting to be told. And your client may or may not be ready to tell it. And you, the practitioner, will need to hear the story. This, too, can be difficult.

Traumatic experiences may call into question, both for the practitioner and the client, everything they believe to be true: That people are inherently good. That good things happen to good people. That we can protect ourselves and our families from harm. That life is fair.

Traumatic experiences happen in spite of us believing that they should not. And more often than not they don't just *happen*. Much trauma is related to what people do to each other. Children are hurt by their parents. Spouses hurt each other. In other words, there is often an interpersonal component to traumatic experiences. This can make recovery from Posttraumatic stress disorder difficult. If your client has been hurt by someone close, it can be difficult to enter into a new relationship—and that includes the therapeutic relationship. For the treatment provider, this can be frustrating. You may know exactly what you need to do but find that your client can't let her guard down.

Also keep in mind that clients who come from historically marginalized populations—such as those subjected to broad-scale, historical trauma—may have suffered relational (and actual) injuries that can make it very difficult for them to believe that any one person or institution can be trusted at all.

And if your client can't let her guard down, she may not be able to tell her story in a meaningful way. The relationship between you and your client becomes the "container," the safe holding environment, for your client's story. People "break" in relationships, but they also heal in relationships. Treatment for posttraumatic stress disorder is more than the transmission of knowledge about trauma, symptoms, and coping skills. Treatment for posttraumatic stress disorder communicates, carefully and humbly, that

- there are good people who will help;
- good things can still happen;

- protecting oneself and each other is a noble task, and so is helping those who are hurt to heal;
- safe spaces can be created, and relationships can be safe.

A Word about Self-Care

It is not only clients who can experience a loss of meaning and purpose after being exposed to traumatic experiences. Practitioners, too, need to guard against loss of meaning and purpose.

Practitioners need to be empathic, to feel with and for the client. This can be an exhausting experience. Our clients' traumatic experiences can get to us. Because of this, we need to build and maintain our own safe spaces and relationships. Trauma cannot be everywhere. We need to identify ways in which we can truly go home after work and accept that the work of the day is done (knowing that there is more to be done the next day).

What this means is that as practitioners we:

- need to have a life outside of work. We should be doing things we love and be around people we care about and who care about us—not just because we need to recover from the day's work, but also because helping professionals, too, deserve to live full lives.

- need to accept, humbly, that we cannot mend everything and everyone. There will always be more work to be done.

- need to be a part of, and build, caring and safe families and communities of all kinds.

Supervisors and supervision play an important role in helping practitioners develop and maintain the ability to bear witness to traumatic stories and become agents of change in their clients' lives. Supervision can become the "holding environment" for difficult stories and a source of support for the practitioner. A form of supervision called Reflective Supervision can be particularly helpful with this. To learn more about Reflective Supervision, read *A Practical Guide to Reflective Supervision*, edited by Sherryl Scott Heller and Linda Gilkerson (2009).

The following assessment tools may be helpful in assessing a practitioner's quality of life and self-care, and may provide a basis for discussion in supervision:

- Professional Quality of Life Scale (ProQol): Visit www.proqol.org for a free, current version

- Self-Care Assessment Worksheet adapted by the American University Counseling Center

Learning About the Treatment of Posttraumatic Stress Disorder (PTSD)

This manual is intended to help you learn about the basics of treatment of posttraumatic stress disorder. If you would like to go a step further and learn more, the following materials can be of use.

For a concise introduction into clinical practice guidelines for treating posttraumatic stress disorder, read *Clinical Practice Guideline for the Treatment of PTSD* by the American Psychological Association. This American Psychological Association publication (2017) summarizes the current practices recommended for the treatment of PTSD as well as those that are not. These practice guidelines cover treatment modalities for adults only, not children.

Additionally, you may want to read the *Evidence Summary Screening and Treatment for Posttraumatic Stress Disorder (PTSD)* from SAMHSA's National Registry of Evidence-based Programs and Practices.

If you would like a more in-depth overview of the theoretical foundations of cognitive behavioral therapy (CBT), as well as step-by step practice guidelines integrated with case examples and theoretical musings, you may want to read the following books:

- *Evidence-Based Practice of Cognitive Behavioral Therapy* by Deborah Dobson and Keith S. Dobson

- *Doing CBT: A Comprehensive Guide to Working with Behaviors, Thoughts, and Emotions* by David Tolin

If you are looking for a book outlining evidence-based practices for the treatment of complex traumatic stress disorders, try these books edited by Christine A. Courtois and Julian D. Ford:

- *Treating Complex Traumatic Stress Disorders: Scientific Foundations and Therapeutic Models*

- Child and Adolescent treatment: *Treating Complex Traumatic Stress Disorders in Children and Adolescents: Scientific Foundations and Therapeutic Models*

Additional resources can be found at the International Society for Traumatic Stress Studies website: www.istss.org.

Why Cognitive Behavioral Therapy?

Cognitive behavioral therapy and other forms of cognitive therapy, such as cognitive processing therapy, cognitive therapy, and prolonged exposure therapy, are currently recommended by the American Psychological Association (2017) as the treatments of choice for adults with posttraumatic stress disorder. These treatments have the strongest empirical evidence.

This means that when you are working with adults who suffer from PTSD, you should offer cognitive behavioral therapy to them and explain why. If you are not using a form of cognitive behavioral therapy for the treatment of PTSD, you should be able to explain why (perhaps your client has declined), and you should make a note of this in your client's chart, indicating that you have offered CBT to the client and he or she has declined. You should still incorporate into treatment those elements of CBT your client is willing to accept.

Conceptually, CBT offers a structured approach to treatment. This can create a "counterweight" to the chaos, confusion, and despair that posttraumatic stress disorder can bring. When there seems no way out and change seems impossible, CBT always offers a next step because it insists on clear goals, a structure for each session, and a structure for the course of treatment.

Cognitive Behavioral Therapy Plus

Traditional cognitive behavioral therapy can be "dry" in that it focuses on changing automatic thoughts and cognitive distortions, including faulty core beliefs. Although changing faulty core beliefs that are trauma-based can be very helpful, many of our community-based clients, children and adults alike, need more than just the traditional elements of cognitive behavioral therapy.

There is a newer, more integrative way of doing CBT. An example would be Tolin's (2016) approach. Tolin integrates elements of mindfulness practice, case management, psychoeducation, and a more thoughtful approach to the therapeutic relationship. Traditional forms of CBT have not disregarded the therapeutic relationship, but it would be fair to say that they have not elaborated extensively on the importance of it. This may be due to the dominance of the Cartesianism in Western philosophical thought. We often do believe that we are because we think.

Descartes first asserted this primacy of thought in 1637. Since then his way of thinking of the mind as separate from and superior to the body has become deeply ingrained into our systems of thought, including the ways we understand mental illness. Traditional CBT is an example of this. According to traditional CBT, faulty thinking is to blame for a variety of psychological problems, such as depression and anxiety. CBT Plus asserts the importance of relationship. We learn how to think and feel in our first relationships, and our first relationships even build our moral universe (Narváez, 2014). The therapeutic relationship not only mirrors our first relationships but also creates a corrective experience.

Symptoms of PTSD tell us, loudly, that we are much more than our thoughts. We are a body-mind system, and when the body is suffering, the mind suffers, too. We can try to examine the mind and the body separately, but in practice we are body-mind beings. Because the whole person has been hurt, relationship is needed to help the whole person heal. When the source of hurt is another person, understanding the importance of the therapeutic relationship as a source of healing becomes even more important.

Because of this, attention must be paid, consciously and clearly, to the body and the mind.

At OhioGuidestone, we practice CBT Plus, adding the following elements to more traditional forms of CBT:

- a clear focus on the therapeutic relationship, attachment relationships, and affect regulation based on the theoretical foundation of the field of interpersonal neurobiology, namely the work of Allan Schore (2007, 2016);

- a focus on regulating body processes related to the impact of trauma, namely the work of Van Der Kolk (2014);

- an awareness of *therapy interfering conditions* such as poverty, racism, sexism, and toxic stress, and the integration of this awareness into our treatment model through services that wrap around the client. These services address more than the client's psychological symptoms related to PTSD. Specifically, they address the impact of therapy interfering conditions in our client's lives.

    o Case management services

    o Psychotherapy for PTSD and related symptoms

    o Substance use disorder (SUD) targeted case management

    o Intense outpatient services

    o Therapeutic behavioral services (TBS)

    o Psychosocial rehabilitation (PSR)

    o Psychiatric services

    o Peer recovery

- Integration of "third-wave" cognitive therapy principles such as ACT and DBT.

- Structured, stage-based treatment that takes into account that stages of treatment may need to be revisited. We call this the amoeba model of treatment. This model acknowledges that symptoms of PTSD may wax, wane, and re-occur, and that this is part of the process of PTSD treatment (and not the client's fault).

The therapeutic relationship constitutes the umbrella under which the stages of treatment take place. Of course, lots of things happen in a client's life outside of treatment and impact treatment (and vice versa). Life is messy, and when trauma comes into play, this can be even more true.

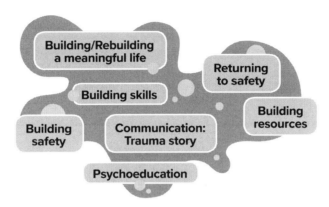

Figure 1

When using the amoeba model, work consciously and openly with your client to clarify what you are doing together. Here are some things you may want to say:

- *We are going to begin by making sure that you are safe.*

- *Feeling unsafe can re-occur. When it does, there is no need to be ashamed. This is just how trauma symptoms work.*

- *It's important to know how trauma may impact you. Let's work on learning about the impact of trauma today.*

- *Telling your story is part of getting better. In what way are you ready to tell your story? In what way are you not yet ready? What part of your story are you ready to tell now? What part are you not ready to tell yet?*

- *Trauma may have robbed you of your ability to do things for yourself and with others. Let's work on getting some of those skills back.*

- *No one should have to do things all alone. Let's work on getting you connected with helpful people and resources.*

- *Let's start thinking about the life you want to build.*

A linear treatment model would conceptualize stages of treatment like this:

Figure 2

The trouble with a linear treatment model for PTSD is that it can negate the complexities of living with PTSD and of trauma treatment. Your client may think that once he has established a sense of safety he should have mastered being safe, and he may feel like a failure when he doesn't. This way of thinking is not helpful for your client or for you.

Community Mental Health Practice Alert:

The Treatment of Clients with Posttraumatic Stress Disorder and Concurrent Substance Use Disorders

In community mental health it is rare to see a client who struggles with just one issue. Many of our clients come to us after years of struggle. Berenz and Coffey (2012) noted that "approximately half of the individuals seeking SUD treatment meet criteria for current PTSD" (p. 469).

Practitioners often note that our clients are facing traumatic experiences and are self-medicating, and that substance abuse can lead to further traumatic experiences due to a loss of control over one's actions. Because many clients who are diagnosed with PTSD also struggle with substance abuse, you must always assess a client with PTSD for a concurrent substance use disorder and, if present, both disorders should be treated concurrently.

The APA Treatment Guidelines (American Psychiatric Association, 2013) did not include the evaluation of treatment modalities for those who suffer from PTSD *and* a substance use disorder. There was disagreement within the APA panel as to whether treatment guidelines should be applied to those suffering from both PTSD and substance use disorders.

What then, should the informed practitioner do when treating clients with both PTSD and a concurrent substance use disorder?

- Use treatment modalities that solidly incorporate elements of CBT while providing best practice treatment for SUDs.

- Provide a wrap-around approach to treatment. Your client may need therapeutic support in the form of CBT-based treatment, psychiatric treatment such as medication assisted treatment (MAT), and case management services to address problems such as homelessness that could greatly impact both PTSD and SUD symptoms.

Here is a list of services your client with concurrent PTSD and SUD may need:

- individual counseling to address PTSD and substance abuse

- therapeutic behavioral services (TBS) to address PTSD-related problems in daily life

- psychosocial rehabilitation (PSR)

- SUD-targeted case management

- psychiatry

- peer recovery

Seeking Safety: A Treatment Manual for PTSD and Substance Abuse by Lisa M. Najavits is a treatment curriculum that incorporates elements of cognitive behavioral therapy in the concurrent treatment of PTSD and substance use disorder and is currently recommended for the treatment of PTSD with a concurrent substance use disorder by the Society for Clinical Psychology.

The *Seeking Safety* curriculum may be particularly suited for many of our community mental health clients. It focuses throughout treatment on the establishment and maintenance of safety. Because the focus is on safety in the present, prolonged exposure, a common CBT treatment modality, is not a part of the treatment protocol.

Prolonged exposure carries a risk for clients who also abuse substances. A client who has not acquired sufficient coping skills to manage intense feelings brought on by exposure to a past traumatic event can become overwhelmed. This client may then be at greater risk for abusing substances.

If your client is able to maintain safety over long periods of time (has met the goals of the *Seeking Safety* curriculum), you may want to consider beginning with exposure therapy in a careful manner. Najavits is currently working on expanding the *Seeking Safety* treatment curriculum to include a past-focused (exposure) component to be called *Creating Change*.

For more information about Seeking Safety and Creating Change, visit www.treatment-innovations.org/.

What About Very Young Children?

This manual does not cover the treatment of very young children. For children from birth to age five, consider using child parent psychotherapy (CPP), which is rated by the California Evidence-Based Clearinghouse for Child Welfare as "supported by research evidence" with a high child welfare relevance score. For more information about CPP's evidence-based rating visit www.cebc4cw.org/program/child-parent-psychotherapy/detailed.

What About Children?

For older children, the evidence points to the use of altered forms of cognitive behavioral therapy for the treatment of PTSD. Ford and Cloitre (2009) pointed to trauma-focused cognitive behavioral therapy (TF-CBT) as the evidence-based treatment modality of choice.

TF-CBT adds developmentally appropriate components to CBT and acknowledges that treatment for a child with PTSD should include the primary caretaker. TF-CBT is short-term, structured treatment that includes many components you should already be familiar with, such as an initial focus on establishing safety, parent and child psychoeducation, coping-skill building, a parenting component, and the telling (in some way) of the trauma story (Cohen, et al., 2016). As such, TF-CBT is similar to other stages-based treatment of PTSD for adults.

For more information about TF-CBT you may want to read SAMHSA's description of TF-CBT at www.nrepp.samhsa.gov/ProgramProfile.aspx?id=96.

While TF-CBT is the most studied of CBT-based treatment models for children with PTSD, it is not always practical to use TF-CBT in the community mental health setting. At OhioGuidestone we choose to use CBT for the treatment of children with PTSD in developmentally appropriate ways, augmenting more traditional forms of CBT in ways that make it accessible for children and their caretakers.

Using developmentally appropriate forms of CBT for the treatment of PTSD in children works in the community mental health setting. Treatment for children with PTSD should:

- be CBT-based;

- include the primary caretaker;

- have a parenting component to help the primary caretaker manage the child's emotional and behavioral problems related to the trauma;

- begin with establishing the child's safety;

- be developmentally appropriate;

- address damage to primary attachment relationships;

- provide psychoeducation about trauma and the impact of trauma;

- incorporate coping skill building;

- incorporate education and skill building about calming the body;

- foster the telling (in some way) of the trauma story;

- incorporate the child's way of being and communicating using art and play; and

- help the child and caretaker move beyond traumatic experiences toward building a full life.

The American Psychological Association (APA) has not yet established treatment guidelines for children with PTSD equivalent to those recently published for adults in 2017.

Many of the children we treat for PTSD have experienced more than one traumatic incident. Trauma and toxic stress may be so embedded in their lives that their reality is shaped by these forces. In other words, experiences of trauma and toxic stress are fundamental to their development.

The terms *developmental and complex trauma* and *toxic stress* adequately describe what we often face in the community mental health setting. Treatment outcomes are likely to be less "miraculous" for children and adults who have been exposed to developmental and complex trauma as well as toxic stress. There is a significant need for future research that includes these populations. In the real world of community mental health treatment, conditions often overlap and make treatment more complex.

Treatment for children and adults who have suffered developmental and complex trauma will, by nature, be more complex and longer-term. This does not mean that symptom reduction can't be achieved through shorter-term treatment. But complex symptoms, such as altered attachment patterns and extensive difficulties with affect regulation leading to further interpersonal difficulties and difficulties in functioning, require longer-term treatment.

CBT: The Essential Elements

CBT focuses on addressing the three elements of the cognitive triad: thoughts (also known as cognitions), feelings (also known as emotions), and behaviors. Why is it called the cognitive triad and not the feelings or emotional triad? Ultimately, CBT holds that all kinds of problems, be they behavioral or emotional, are rooted in unrealistic and faulty thinking. Hence, unrealistic and faulty thinking must be identified and corrected.

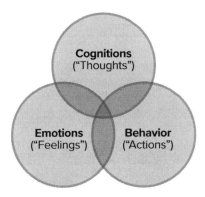

Figure 3

This conceptualization contains three components:

- the cognitive component
- the emotional component
- the behavioral component

These three interact with each other. The cognitive component, which we can refer to as thoughts, includes automatic thoughts. These are thoughts that just "happen." Tolin (2016) calls them "interpretations" because they usually interpret what is happening in some unpleasant way. Thoughts impact behaviors and emotions. But behaviors also impact emotions and thoughts.

Symptoms of posttraumatic stress disorder have the potential to impact all three elements of the cognitive triad:

- Trauma can change the way you think. You may adopt a negative and fearful way of thinking about yourself and the world.
- Trauma can impact the way you feel. You may feel depressed, anxious, sad, angry, or frustrated much of the time.

- Trauma can impact the things you do. You may become hypervigilant, act aggressively, withdraw from the world, or dissociate.

What Exactly Do We Mean When We Talk About the Cognitive Component?

What and how we think impacts how we feel and what we do. But do we always know what we are thinking? Beck et al. (1979) observed that people who suffer from depression are in constant debate with their own persistent and unwanted negative thoughts. He used the metaphor of an intercom to bring this internal chatter into the therapeutic conversation. Beck named this uninvited, ever-present chatter "automatic thoughts." These are the thoughts we did not ask for and are often only somewhat aware of.

- "I always mess everything up."
- "She hates me."
- "I am going to fail."

Notice that automatic thoughts are judgmental in nature. They don't compliment us. If they do, they are not problematic and seldom a topic in treatment. It would be a good idea to track the transformation from negative automatic thoughts to more realistic thoughts in the course of treatment.

Here are some examples of automatic thoughts your client with PTSD may experience:

- "It's me. It's always me. There is nothing I can do about it."
- "My life is ruined."
- "No one is going to want me after this."

But Where Do These Automatic Thoughts Originate?

In CBT, basic negative views of self, others, and the world are called "core beliefs" or "schemas." We may hold these beliefs without being aware of them. They drive how we think about ourselves consciously and unconsciously, each other, and the world. Automatic thoughts are rooted in core beliefs. For the most part, we are not aware of the core beliefs we hold.

Here are some examples of core beliefs:

- "I am unworthy."
- "I am a failure."
- "I am unlovable."

Your clients with PTSD may have core beliefs specifically related to the trauma they have experienced, such as a child who was repeatedly abused by her parents holding the core belief that she is unlovable. Her experience was that she was not loved; hence her core belief has become that she is unlovable. This belief is, in some ways, self-protective. If she believes that she is unlovable, then she will most likely not be disappointed by a lack of love she presently experiences.

These, of course, are examples of unhealthy core beliefs. Here are some examples of healthy core beliefs:

- "I am worthy."
- "I am capable."
- "I am lovable."

Where, Then, Do These Core Beliefs Come From?

CBT insists on focusing on the here and now. We may never know where our core beliefs come from. Or, in the case of a client who experienced extensive developmental trauma, we may know, but knowing whom to blame for core beliefs doesn't help us deconstruct them. Yes, perhaps a parent instilled a sense of worthlessness that led to a core belief of unworthiness. But CBT is what Tolin (2016) calls "present oriented" (p. 8). It is not that CBT discredits what has happened to a client or disregards the emotional pain that the past may have caused; rather, CBT insists that the client move into the here and now. The question to our client then becomes:

- "What do you think/believe about what happened to you?"
- "Are there other, more realistic and accurate ways of thinking about the past/ the impact of the past?"

In other words, CBT Plus asserts that these beliefs and thoughts are changed in the context of the safe therapeutic relationship. In other words, core beliefs and automatic thoughts have a context and are changed in the context of the safe holding environment of the therapeutic relationship.

A client who was neglected by her parents and emotionally and sexually abused holds the core belief that she is "ruined for life." Her automatic thoughts tell her that she is "dirty" and that no one would want her. CBT would acknowledge the hurt but move toward correcting those faulty automatic thoughts about being dirty, using evidence from the here and now.

CBT insists that we examine the core belief using empirical methods, then adjust to a more realistic one. More adaptive and realistic core beliefs then lead to more adaptive and realistic thoughts that correct negative automatic thoughts. More realistic thoughts about self, other, and the world lead to behaviors that are a better fit for reality and hence produce better outcomes.

Clients who have been repeatedly traumatized may have to battle a multitude of negative automatic thoughts daily. It may be helpful to think of those negative automatic thoughts as little intruders that can be greeted and disarmed. But keep in mind that your client may be so used to negative automatic thoughts that they may seem completely rational. Additionally, consider that it may not be helpful to call these beliefs "faulty." They may have served a protective function!

The core belief "I am unlovable" can "protect" your client from disappointment. Negative core beliefs can be adaptive in their own way, but this does not mean that they are the best and most appropriate beliefs your client can hold.

Here is how thoughts (cognitions) are viewed in CBT:

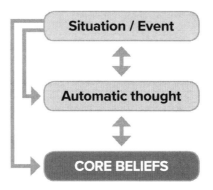

Figure 4: Note that core beliefs are much harder to identify than automatic thoughts. ATs just appear. We do not have to ask for them. Because they appear so often, they are easier to bring into conscious awareness.

An event or situation triggers a core belief. The core belief results in negative automatic thoughts. These negative automatic thoughts lead to behaviors that are not a good fit with the situation because they are faulty interpretations of what is actually going on.

Here is an example of what this may look like: Jason is having an argument with his partner. As soon as the disagreement begins, he hears himself saying to himself: "Stupid, I am so stupid." This automatic thought is rooted in Jason's core belief that he is unlovable. He developed this core belief as a young child due to ongoing emotional neglect.

Jason is overwhelmed by both sadness and anger (the emotional component of the cognitive triad) and lashes out at his partner, then leaves (the behavioral component of the triad). What went wrong?

Jason did not assess the situation accurately. He is clearly not "stupid" (finished high schools, works as a mechanic). But he does have a core belief that he is unlovable (clearly also not true, as he is currently in a loving relationship). He reacts emotionally to his negative automatic thoughts, and his actions are based on the intense emotions of sadness and anger. The key in Jason's treatment is to get him away from faulty interpretations into more accurate interpretations of what is truly happening right now. Here is what that might look like:

Jason comes to understand that disagreements are a normal part of any relationship. He recognizes his sadness about having a disagreement, but he moves past this and tries to work out a compromise with his partner. When he reaches a compromise, he feels validated, competent, and loved.

Here is an example of the impact of trauma-based negative automatic thoughts and core beliefs:

Ty was severely neglected by his biological mother due to her extensive drug abuse. When he was removed from her care at age three, he was malnourished, and it was discovered that he had been sexually abused by an acquaintance of his mother's. When Ty entered school, he did not get along with his peers. He often played alone and did not make friends. As an adult, Ty continues to struggle with relationships. He also frequently shoplifts and engages in casual sexual encounters. Here are some of the automatic thoughts he reports:

- "Got to get that, quick."
- "This won't last."
- "Got to take care of number one."

These automatic thoughts make sense when you consider Ty's experiences. His experiences have told him that:

- He needs to quickly get what he can because no one else will take care of his needs.
- Things and people disappear quickly.
- He has to take care of himself because no one else will.

Here are some core beliefs Ty developed:

- "I am unworthy of love and attention."
- "The strong take care of themselves. Everyone else goes under."
- "The ends justify the means."
- "Everyone stands alone."

If you find yourself repeatedly talking with your client about a pesky automatic thought, you may be on to a core belief.

What About Behaviors? What Do We Mean When We Refer to the Behavioral Component of Posttraumatic Stress Disorder?

Inaccurate core beliefs lead to inaccurate automatic thoughts about a situation. These automatic, negative, and rapid-fire thoughts lead to behavioral responses that are based on a faulty assessment of the situation. If I assume that things will go wrong no matter what I do, my assessment of the future will be negative, and I may conclude that there is no need for me to act purposefully and consciously. Why should I act at all if nothing matters, or if everything I do goes wrong? Inaction then leads to more faulty assessments of the present situation.

Additionally, your client may act a lot in ways that do not fit the current situation. If nothing matters, you may act in ways that are random. If nothing you do matters, then you may steal from your parents to support a drug addiction.

Note that a main behavioral component of posttraumatic stress disorder is multifaceted mirroring of the many symptoms of PTSD. PTSD symptoms translate into PTSD-related behaviors. You client may become withdrawn, avoidant, and inactive. Your client may also act in ways that do not make sense to others due to dissociative symptoms. Or your client may be hyper-vigilantly aggressive. Many of our clients alternate between these kinds of behavioral responses to PTSD symptoms.

Behavioral Activation

Behaviors based on faulty interpretations of self, others, and the world maintain PTSD symptoms. In order to address those symptoms, behaviors must change. In CBT this is called "behavioral activation." When using behavioral activation, we help our clients realize that "doing better in order to feel better" (Tolin, 2016, p. 39) can work. Here is how behaviors (actions) are viewed in CBT:

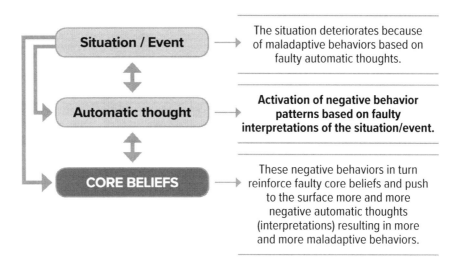

Figure 5

Here is how this may look for your client with PTSD:

Sarah is plagued by negative automatic thoughts about herself. She constantly tells herself that nothing will ever change, that she is stupid and only has herself to blame for her situation. These automatic thoughts behaviorally "paralyze" her. As a result, she rarely leaves her apartment, and this makes her feel even worse about herself. Thoughts of worthlessness dominate her thinking, dictate the way she feels about herself, and drive her to spend her days in front of the television watching soap operas.

What About the Emotional Component of the Cognitive Triad?

What are emotions? Why do we have them? Tolin (2016) acknowledges that basic human emotions are biologically based and serve a function. Fear, for example, evolutionarily speaking, is meant to keep us alive. So is love. He differentiates between "physiological sensations" and "subjective emotional states" (Tolin, p. 81). In other words: There are basic emotions that we need. They keep us alive. And to be alive means to be connected with others. This is why PTSD is so damaging.

Beck et al. (1979) asserts that depression diminishes or prevents the experience of love and joy (p. 35). All that is left, then, are unpleasant or seemingly intolerable emotional experiences such as rage, anger, and despair. PTSD gives us similar messages.

PTSD tells us that we are alone, that others are dangerous and will hurt us. Neurobiologically, in order to be well, we need to be connected to a caring community. We need to be a part of a group. But once you have been significantly hurt by others, being with others becomes risky. How would we be able to tell that the group is safe?

When this connection to others and to a safe community is broken or feels broken (as it does in PTSD), our emotions become a "subjective emotional state" disconnected from a collective emotional state, further reinforcing loneliness and helplessness (Tolin, 2016, p. 81).

Emotions are impacted by physiological states. A racing heart can trigger the emotion of fear. For those with PTSD, a racing heart can also trigger a hypervigilant state of mind and body. They are ready to fight or flee, whichever the situation calls for. The trouble for those who suffer from PTSD is that almost any seemingly random trigger can initiate the fight/flight response. If the situation seems hopeless, a freeze response can occur.

Depending on the physiological state and emotional response to the trigger, your client may feel hopeless, agitated, or aggressive, and act on these emotions in ways that do not make sense to others.

Emotions, behaviors, automatic thoughts—and ultimately core beliefs—are intimately connected, always interacting with each other. Emotions can be adaptive when they move us into the right kind of action. Here is an example: If someone in my family dies, I will naturally feel sad. There may be a physical feeling of heaviness or, in the case of a sudden and unexpected loss, a sense of shock. This feeling of heaviness and sadness is meant, neurobiologically, to send me back into the company of my family or friends.

If I reconnect with my group because I am sad, the sadness is adaptive. If I stay in extended isolation, my sadness may increase, turning into depression and the feeling that no one can understand. If no one understands me, then there is no need to go out and connect with others. I am alone in my suffering. Surely this feeling reinforces my depression.

Here is how this may look for your client with PTSD:

Ria has been through a series of violent relationships. She has recently separated from her partner, who is now stalking her. Ria's two young children are both very close to her, but they sometimes fear her, because Ria easily flies off the handle.

When there is a loud sound, Ria winces and immediately feels helpless and hopeless. She often runs and hides in her bedroom when she hears the mailman drop the mail into the mail slot.

At other times Ria flies off the handle when her youngest child cries. She becomes aggressive, both verbally and physically, and swats her daughter to "shut her up." Ria's emotional response is feelings of anger and rage.

Ria's emotional responses of helplessness, hopelessness, anger, and rage are expressions of her PTSD symptoms. Her emotional responses are, contextually speaking, protective: Loud sounds may mean harm is coming; hence the children will have to be silenced quickly to avoid further hurt.

Note that feelings of helplessness and rage are not mutually exclusive. They simply represent different ways of responding to a perceived threat.

Here is how the emotional components of depression relate to the behavioral and cognitive components:

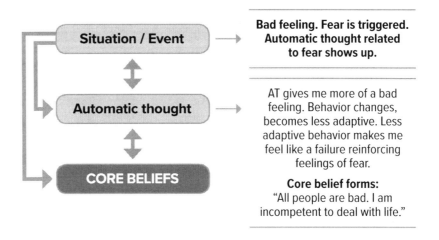

Figure 6

CBT in Action: How to Conceptualize a Case

CBT offers a clear path to treatment in that it insists that after a thorough assessment, you must develop a clear case formulation (Dobson & Dobson, 2017). Tolin (2016) calls this a "meaty conceptualization" (p. 94) of your case. In other words: We must create a hypothesis of what is creating and maintaining the problem.

When a client presents with symptoms of PTSD, you should strive to understand the specific trauma your client went through. This can be difficult in the beginning of the therapeutic relationship, as your client may not be fully ready to share the story. Sometimes it can be helpful to obtain information about your client's trauma from others, if your client agrees to this. Be sure to obtain a signed consent for Release of Information (ROI).

While trauma can have a tremendous impact on a person's life, if would be a mistake to automatically attribute all of your client's symptoms to the traumatic experience. You should find out what your client's baseline functioning was. It's quite possible that your client struggled with mental health problems before the traumatic event.

Once you have completed your case conceptualization, you are ready to identify your intervention targets and create a treatment plan. But first you must put your case conceptualization on paper. Where does it go?

- Your case conceptualization belongs in the Clinical Summary Section of the Diagnostic Evaluation I (in Evolv). When you write your Clinical Summary, be sure to include the situational, behavioral, emotional, and cognitive elements that create and maintain your client's problems. Also, name what problems you want to target with your client. The problems you have identified become the basis of your treatment plan.

- If you have identified trauma as the cause of your client's symptoms, you would choose the problem category "Trauma" (in Evolv) to form the basis of your client's treatment plan.

Here is an example of why case conceptualization is important.

You are working with Lee, who is perpetually in motion. His third-grade teacher calls you and explains that Lee is "hyperactive" and asks if you could refer Lee to a psychiatrist so that he can receive medication for "his ADHD."

When you meet with Lee and his mother, she describes Lee as a great kid whose development was perfectly normal until his father began using methamphetamines. The father, who no longer lives in the home, picked on Lee, called him names, and slapped him around. Additionally, Lee witnessed his mother being assaulted many times. During those times Lee had reason to believe that his mother would die.

Even though Lee's father left the family more than two years ago, Lee is still watchful at all times. He paces the perimeter of the apartment while you are there, looking out the window often and checking to make sure the door is locked. Lee can't sleep at night and may yell at anyone, even strangers, who appears to threaten his mother.

In context, Lee's behavior makes sense. Lee seems stuck in hypervigilant and anxious behaviors that look like hyperactivity but are actually expressions of his PTSD symptoms. Etiology matters. In this case, working with Lee and his mother on overcoming their trauma symptoms will reduce his restlessness, which is really anxiousness and hypervigilance.

It is important to inquire about baseline functioning. If Lee had displayed the same behaviors before his traumatic experiences began, he may have had a hyper-activity disorder to begin with, which would then have been exacerbated by his traumatic experiences.

Let's walk through a case:

Case Vignette: Chantelle

Chantelle is a 26-year-old African-American woman who lives in the Central neighborhood of Cleveland with her three young children, all under the age of six. Chantelle lives in public housing and worries about her family's safety every day. She hears gunshots often and not only at night.

Chantelle was struck by a stray bullet three months ago. Her children all witnessed the shooting. After undergoing surgery to remove the bullet from her abdomen, she spent several days in the hospital. When Chantelle returned home, she was understandably fearful of leaving the house. Her children did not want to leave her side.

Chantelle really wants to move but can't afford to. At night, she gathers her children in the center of the apartment where they all sleep on a mattress; she is afraid a bullet will pierce an exterior wall and strike her or one of her children. Neither Chantelle nor her children get much sleep. Chantelle blames herself for her children witnessing her being shot as she now feels she should not have she stepped out of the house at dusk.

Chantelle is often "snappy" with her children and recently got into an altercation with a neighbor. As a result of this altercation, Chantelle now refuses to leave the house at all. Her house is in disarray. Her curtains are always drawn. Chantelle spends her days sitting in bed and staring into space or watching TV. She feels that she can't ever be happy or safe again. When she does sleep, she suffers from nightmares. Chantelle refuses to speak with anyone about the shooting.

Chantelle's case is not an uncommon one. Our clients are often faced with multiple barriers, many of which are beyond their control. Let's call them therapy interfering conditions:

- poverty
- lack of education
- incarceration of a family member
- disability
- racism

Our clients did not choose these conditions, but they are forced to deal with them. There is ample evidence that conditions of toxic stress, especially in childhood, can contribute to the development of physical and mental illness. For further information about the relationship between adverse childhood experiences and the development of physical and mental illness you may want to read articles referenced on the Aces Too High website: www.acestoohigh.com.

How can CBT be helpful when there are therapy interfering conditions present?

- CBT can help correct automatic thoughts of self-blame about conditions beyond the client's control.

- CBT can help the client focus on taking action. Moving into action can take many forms, including advocating for social justice.

- CBT can help the client take action for herself/himself, moving from helplessness to self-efficacy.

Community Mental Health Practice Alert

Chantelle lives in poverty, as many of our clients do. She has few external resources. She does not have a car. She does not have savings. Her support system is crumbling. Access to healthy foods is limited.

Your case conceptualization must incorporate the conditions Chantelle lives in. They have shaped her way of thinking and being and her way of responding to being shot.

Including conditions of toxic stress in the case conceptualization helps to show Chantelle that not everything is her fault. Incorporating conditions of toxic stress also incorporates a behavioral component into Chantelle's treatment. When Chantelle is ready to do so, she may want to take value-based action and develop or increase her advocacy for herself and others living in poverty.

In other words: Chantelle would learn to take action again. Taking action to create change is a behavior we want to increase through the use of CBT. Keep in mind that the behavior of taking action will have to be modeled and taught.

Let's try this for our client Chantelle:

Chantelle: Assessment and Case Conceptualization/ Problem Identification

Use the Diagnostic Evaluation Part 1 and Part 2. Include information about Chantelle's socioeconomic status, including her living conditions, in the DE. Here is what your Clinical Summary (case conceptualization) may look like:

Chantelle was recently shot and seriously harmed by a stray bullet. Her injuries were life threatening, and she required surgery and hospitalization. The shooting took place in Chantelle's neighborhood, and the shooter was never identified. Chantelle has always lived in poverty, but she has been resourceful and able to take care of her children.

Since the shooting, Chantelle has suffered from nightmares and lack of sleep. She blames herself for the shooting and her children having to witness it. As a result, Chantelle is often upset, angry, and withdrawn. She avoids going outside as well as talking about the shooting. Chantelle reports that she feels she can't ever be happy again. She is completely inactive and has gained 30 pounds since the incident.

Problems:

1. Cognitive: Cognitive errors, feels she can't ever be happy again, self-blame for the shooting, thinks that talking about the shooting will make things worse for her.

2. Behavioral: Basic self-care is lacking—poor nutrition, sleeping too much, not taking care of fundamentals, lack of meaningful and joyful interaction with her children, not taking any steps to improve her situation.

3. Emotional: Anxiety, hopelessness, anger.

What, then, would be a good goal for Chantelle? Overall, the goal that most fits Chantelle from the Evolv Library is:

Reduce Trauma Symptoms

Note that the problem list does not encompass all of Chantelle's problems, but rather focuses on what is most important. We would want to focus on the behavioral components of treatment first: Better sleep, better nutrition, better medical care, and improved stability are likely to impact Chantelle's symptoms.

You have completed your case conceptualization. This is a good time to check in with your client.

Ask:

- *Did I get this right?*

- *Is there anything I left out?*

- *Is there anything I need to add?*

Make sure that you are working collaboratively with your client on identifying problems and treatment goals. While CBT can be more directive than other forms of therapy, collaboration ensures a therapeutic alliance and "joint ownership" (Dobson & Dobson, 2017, p. 53). A solid therapeutic alliance and client and therapist ownership of the case formulation, problem identification, and treatment planning form the basis for treatment success.

If you don't work collaboratively, treatment success is jeopardized from the start. You may think that you understand the client's basic problems. You may have a great case conceptualization in your mind. And you may even be correct in the way you conceptualize the case. But if your client disagrees with you, she may never fully participate in treatment. Any goals you have established may be partially irrelevant to her; hence, she may not be committed to the course of treatment you are thinking about, and treatment success becomes questionable.

How can you ensure that you are working collaboratively with your client?

- Ask frequently: *Did I get this right? Is there anything you want to add? What part of what I am saying does not sit right with you?*

- If your client is not ready for the kind of change you have in mind, go back to basics. Ask the miracle question: If you had one wish and it would come true tomorrow morning, what would your wish be (Jong & Berg, 2013)? Build collaboration based on that wish.

- Understand that collaboration and trust are built and that it is your responsibility to model them.

Assessment should encompass all three aspects: thoughts, feelings, and behaviors. It should be collaborative and structured. It should utilize valid standardized measures and lead to a case conceptualization laid out in the clinical summary of the diagnostic evaluation. The Clinical Summary concludes with an identification of problems in order of importance.

Once problems have been identified collaboratively, the treatment plan can be completed.

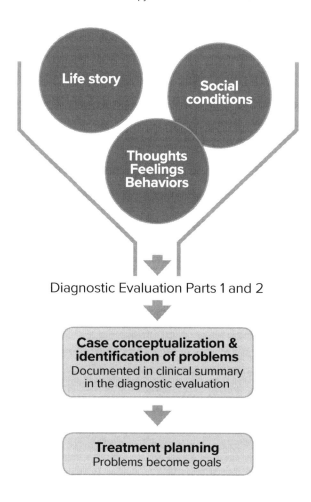

Figure 7

A Word About Suicide/Suicidal Ideation and Safety Planning

If your client discloses thoughts of suicide, complete a formalized suicide risk assessment. Do so in a caring and compassionate manner, stating that you are asking your client these questions because you want her to be well. Document completion of a formal suicide risk assessment in your case notes and ensure that the suicide risk assessment is scanned into the client's electronic record.

Once you have completed the formalized suicide risk assessment, you will in all likelihood need to complete a safety plan. Any safety concerns about a client must also be reported and discussed with your supervisor on the day that they occur.

If your client indicates thoughts of self-harm, this must be noted in the client record as a problem, using the problem category *Safety/Risk of harm to self/others.*

After you have selected the appropriate problem, you must also select an appropriate goal and method. If your client reports risk of harm to self and other, you must treat this problem. Not providing (and documenting) appropriate treatment for suicidal or homicidal ideation puts your client and others at risk.

What Is the Function of a Safety Plan?

Tolin (2016) rightfully points out that safety planning in no way guarantees that your client will not harm herself. But a safety plan denotes to both you and the client the importance of the matter and specifically the importance of taking action.

By collaboratively creating a safety plan with your client, you are:

- expressing genuine concern and compassion. You are expressing that you value your client as a human being and you want her to stay alive so she can create the kind of life she wants to live based on the values she wants to embody.

- modeling immediately the importance of taking positive and life-affirming action. Because PTSD often leads to feelings of hopeless and helplessness, it is important to create this counterweight to the inaction that PTSD can bring with it. CBT calls this "behavior activation" (Tolin, 2016, p. 224).

What Should Be Included in a Safety Plan?

Use the OGS Safety Planning Form to create your safety plan. This form will identify:

- concerning thoughts;

- concerning behaviors;

- things the client can do (behavioral activation to shift attention);

- people the client can talk to (behavioral activation aimed at changing attentional focus to supportive and caring relationships); and

- triggers and removal of triggers from the environment. If medications are a trigger, they should be secured. No person with suicidal thoughts should have access to firearms in the home. Even if they are locked away, the risk of gaining access is there and a plan should be made to temporarily remove them.

Can a Safety Plan Guarantee the Safety of Your Client?

A safety plan cannot guarantee the safety of your client. It does, however, indicate that you and your client have adequately addressed the issue of suicidal thoughts and behaviors and that you, the clinician, have actively taken all appropriate steps to help your client stay safe and alive.

What About Children?

When creating a safety plan with a child, the parent must always be involved. If a child discloses a safety issue and the parent is not present, you must contact the parent immediately (and notify your supervisor). A meeting must be scheduled on the same day to create a safety plan. Remember, safety planning is a collaborative process. A meaningful safety plan addresses the concerns of the parent and the child.

What will not work:

- Meeting with the client and parent with a ready-made safety plan that does not take into account the specific family circumstances.

- Creating a vague safety plan including statements such as "will call a friend" or "parent will put away all medications."

- Things that are impossible, such as "parent will supervise client at all times" when the parent works full time.

What will work:

- Being compassionate and inquisitive about the client's and family's specific circumstances. Learn as much as you can to collaboratively create a workable safety plan.

- Being specific. Outline specifically where the client will go, who the client can call (include phone numbers), and what the client will do. An example of this would be: "Client will build a Lego tower in the kitchen while guardian . . ."

- Things that are possible, such as: "Parent will ensure appropriate supervision of client. Aunt will play Legos with client/go for a walk with client . . ."

Sometimes nothing seems to work. When this is the case, it is important to consider the following factors:

- Is there anything reinforcing the client's need to be hospitalized? In other words, will the client receive more attention and perhaps compassion if she is so ill that she requires hospitalization?

- Does the client need more professional attention? If so, how can that happen? Is a partial hospitalization or day treatment program needed? Some form of respite? When children display behavioral acting out, adults frequently label them as manipulative. Keep in mind that your client may express an actual need. However, your client may not be able to tell you (yet) what she needs. This in itself is a clinical issue that requires attention.

- If your client is a child: Is the parent simply exhausted from caring for a mentally ill child? Is a more intensive level of service needed? Is respite needed? Does the parent need her own services?

- Is the client/family in a very dysregulated state? Can you assist with helping calm emotions? Can you instill hope that things will get better?

Sometimes hospitalization is needed to stabilize a client. This does not mean that you or the client failed. It does mean that a better plan is needed. It is important to begin with planning for discharge right away. What will be different? What can you do? What can your client do? How can the environment change?

A Word About Suicide Risk and Posttraumatic Stress Disorder

Trauma can call into question everything one holds true and dear. Repeated experiences of trauma, especially interpersonal trauma, can lead to a loss of hope and meaning. Once hope and meaning are lost, thoughts of suicide can take on a life of their own.

When working with clients who have been repeatedly traumatized, you must assess their level of hopelessness, which can result from a loss of meaning and purpose. Trauma treatment must include helping your client find meaning and purpose one day at a time.

Treatment Planning in CBT

Safety always comes first. If your client displays behaviors such as suicidal gestures or actions or severe self-harm that could result in death, these need to be addressed first. There are many ways in which CBT responds to suicidal behaviors. Here are some of them:

- making the environment safe by identifying and removing triggers from the environment;

- changing client behavioral responses to triggers;

- increasing skills to manage triggers and resulting emotional states (skill building); and

- examining and changing automatic thoughts leading to suicidal behaviors.

Is it necessary to address all three elements of the cognitive triad in the treatment plan? What about behavioral interventions for those who struggle with thinking things through?

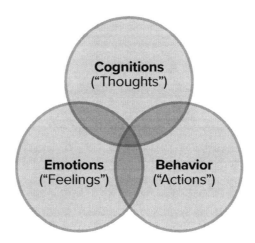

Figure 8: The Cognitive Triad

It is not necessary to address all three elements of the cognitive triad equally and right away. In fact, Tolin (2016), referring to behavioral interventions, recommends that "you should strongly consider using these strategies as the 'main course' in your CBT" (p. 161).

Why Start with Behavioral Interventions?

Generally speaking, interventions targeting behaviors may be more accessible to clients. When your client is stuck in a cycle of negative automatic thoughts, it is helpful to interrupt these thoughts by moving your client into action as inaction or hypervigilance can be PTSD symptoms.

Behavioral interventions can also target those tough-to-treat body symptoms. To help your client calm the body, you may want to refer him to a yoga or tai chi group. A client who can calm himself is better able to reflect, which is crucial to addressing cognitive elements of PTSD such as faulty thinking.

Targeting behavioral symptoms may be the most accessible "door" to treating PTSD. They make sense. When a client is socially isolated, creating a schedule of activities is a logical step. Your client cannot think herself out of her PTSD symptoms. But she can take behavioral action steps that will improve her thinking and the way she feels about herself.

Community Mental Health Practice Alert

Our clients often struggle with basic skills for many reasons.

Therapy Interfering Conditions can lead to skills deficits in people who are otherwise competent. Poverty may lead to an educational impairment. It is difficult to learn when you are hungry or worried about housing. It is difficult to learn when you have to move a lot. If you grew up in an old house and you have been exposed to lead, learning can become a real challenge.

While our clients may have skills deficits, this does not mean that they are incapable of learning. It is not a good idea to underestimate our clients' ability to learn, grow, and overcome.

Psychoeducation and behavioral interventions can be very empowering. The experience of competence is powerful and can lead to further changes in thinking, feeling, and behavior—just the kind of ripple effect we are looking for.

How to Build a CBT Treatment Plan for PTSD

1. Address safety issues first. This includes creating a safety plan right away if one is needed. If you are unsure if one is needed, consult with your supervisor.
2. Include psychoeducation about trauma and the impact of trauma on thoughts, feelings, and behaviors, as well as relationships.
3. Start with behavioral interventions, such as creating a schedule of activities, building real-world skills, and building relationships.
4. Help your client build a way in which the story of the trauma can be told.
5. Address cognitive elements such as automatic thoughts as they occur. Help your client change negative automatic self-talk. If your client has had some success using behavioral interventions, you now have evidence that your client is competent and that things can go well. Help your client use the evidence!
6. Address faulty thinking such as "things need to go well all the time."
7. Be on the lookout for core beliefs and use Socratic questioning (see below) to address faulty core beliefs. Trauma can change your automatic thoughts and your core beliefs.
8. Build resilience!

What Are Socratic Questions?

Tolin (2016) defined Socratic questions as "a way of helping the client arrive at a conclusion by asking carefully worded questions" (p. 159).

Here are some examples of Socratic questions:

- What does this mean to you?

- How did you come to think about the event this way?

- Is there another possible way of thinking about this event?

- How do you know that what you are thinking is true?

Here are some examples of Socratic questions for your client with PTSD:

- In what way has trauma changed the way you feel about yourself?

- What does trauma tell you about the world? About other people?

- What is the evidence that the messages trauma gives you are true? What is the evidence that these messages are not true?

What Socratic questioning is not:

- getting the client to agree with you ("lip service")

- getting the client to think exactly like you

What Socratic questioning is:

Socratic questioning is a process of asking open-ended questions that point your client in the direction of alternative and more realistic ways of thinking about a problem. Socratic questions point in the direction of evidence. They cannot be answered with a simple "yes" or "no." It is up to your client to discover the answers to your Socratic questions and the impact that the newly discovered evidence can have on thinking, feelings, and being.

Can't I just tell my client what is wrong with the way he is thinking?

There is no evidence that telling a client what to think and feel is effective. Just think about yourself: We all want to believe that we're right. We consider evidence, sometimes reluctantly, and adjust our thinking if we trust the source. Our clients are no different. They make changes to their ways of thinking and doing not because we tell them to, but because they come to trust us to help them assess and reconsider. New interpretations and ways of coping emerge in conversation.

The Golden Rule of CBT

Listen compassionately. Then ask questions that point your client in the direction of evidence that can change the way he or she thinks, feels, and behaves.

Chantelle's Treatment Plan

Chantelle's treatment plan will need to address the following problems as identified in her Diagnostic Evaluation and case conceptualization:

- Cognitive: Poor thinking. Blames self. Faulty belief about self, trauma processing.

- Behavioral: Basic self-care is lacking. Poor nutrition. Not leaving the house. Interactions with children are suffering. Freeze and fight response.

- Emotional: Sadness, hopelessness, shame.

Once again, working collaboratively is paramount. If identification of goals is a problem, go back to the miracle question (Jong & Berg, 2013). Ask your client to describe what her life would look like if all of her problems were suddenly gone. What would she be doing? How would she know things were different?

Here are some goals/methods from the Evolv library that adequately address Chantelle's problems and symptoms:

Goal 1: Reduce Trauma Symptoms

Method 1: Client will increase her capacity for self-care behaviors such as grooming, exercise, good nutrition, and engaging in pleasurable activities for reduction of mental health symptoms.

Method 2: Client will develop and/or share trauma narrative to safely explore trauma.

Please note that Chantelle may not be ready to tell her story yet, even with help. You may want to choose another method, such as:

- Client will engage in activities to increase communication skills.

Chantelle may first have to become comfortable with communicating at all before being able to create and share a trauma narrative.

How are you going to know that Chantelle is following her plan/ getting better?

Use a tracking chart to help Chantelle record self-care items, such as eating healthy foods and leaving the house on a daily basis. Help her recognize what she is already doing well and help her do more of that.

Goal 2: Increase mindfulness

Method 1: Client will use mindfulness techniques to create a sense of belonging in the present/decrease dissociation.

Method 2: Client will learn and practice coping skills to self-soothe in everyday situations.

Note that you can begin treatment with just one goal. A treatment plan is a work in progress and should be adjusted as necessary. Ongoing collaboration is the key to successful treatment planning. Say things like:

- *This is your plan.*

- *Is there anything on your plan that we should change?*

- *What is working for you? What is not working?*

What Is the Role of the Therapeutic Relationship in Cognitive Behavioral Therapy?

Beck (1979) stressed that attention must be paid to the therapeutic relationship (p. 27). CBT is more than a set of techniques. Dobson & Dobson (2017) compared the therapeutic relationship to the "vehicle" that drives change (p. 67). Tolin (2016) references Carl Rogers in calling for empathy, genuineness, and unconditional positive regard (p. 11).

But Tolin (2016) also made it clear "that the therapeutic relationship is *necessary*, but not *sufficient*" (p. 138).

You have to attend to the relationship because the relationship drives the change process. If something is wrong in the relationship between the therapist and the client—perhaps a lack of collaboration or trust—then change is unlikely.

Here is a visual representation of the role of the therapeutic relationship in CBT:

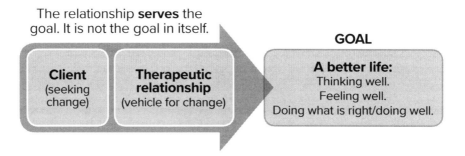

Figure 9

Being Attuned: Building Affect Regulation in the Therapeutic Relationship

Being attuned to your client's emotional state is just as important in CBT as it is in any other form of therapy. Attunement builds the therapeutic relationship.

If your client feels and knows that you are attuned with him, then he is much more likely to trust you. But attunement is not enough in CBT.

Let's take a look at the cognitive triad again:

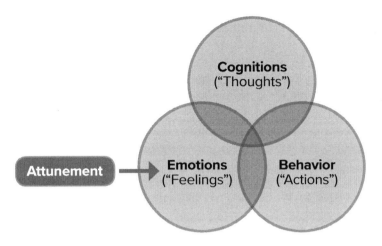

Figure 10

Attunement puts you in touch with your client's emotional state. It gives you an idea how your client feels. You can then better assess what drives his behavior.

You can adjust:

- how you are with your client. You can lower your voice if your client seems agitated and feels threatened but is still unaware of this. You can move your body further away to reduce client feelings of panic/fear.

- what you do with your client: You can offer a blanket or turn on soft music to increase client feelings of safety.

- what you say to your client: You can ask your client if he is feeling threatened/lonely/desperate.

When you are attuning you are working with the emotional component of the cognitive triad. In CBT it is important to always keep in mind how what you are doing fits into the cognitive triad.

Attunement by itself does not "fix" anything. It does help your client feel more comfortable. But if your client feels more comfortable and trusts that you are attuned with him and can handle the complex and intense emotions he is feeling, then he is much more likely to be able to move into action.

If you are attuned with your client, he may be more willing and able to move into work within the cognitive and behavioral component of the cognitive triad. Attunement is an important part of the therapeutic relationship.

What About Co-Regulation? CBT Plus

Co-regulation is a term coined by Allan Schore (2007), the founder of Modern Attachment Theory. Co-regulation is not a CBT term or technique, but understanding co-regulation can be helpful when using CBT. The intentional use of co-regulation differentiates traditional CBT from CBT Plus.

Co-regulation happens when you, the provider, attune with your client. This attunement is initially a right-brain-to-right-brain process, meaning it is a nonverbal and intuitive process. This process happens naturally, though you can intentionally initiate it. To engage in co-regulation you need to intuitively perceive your client's state of mind, connect with this state of mind, and then use your well-regulated state of body and mind to help your client manage her state of body and mind. Your physical and emotional presence impacts the client's physical and emotional presence.

Think about co-regulation in the following way:

When you, the therapist, are upset, your client can sense this upset state of mind and may "take it on." When you are calm, connected, and composed, your client can sense this, too, often without knowing. Communicating a calm, connected, and composed state of mind and body without words is the essence of co-regulation.

Co-regulation is about relationship. It is about truly getting to know, in more than a cognitive way, your client's state of mind and body.

When do I use co-regulation? Co-regulatory processes happen in therapeutic and other relationships all the time. You may want to use co-regulation when your client is not ready or able to consciously and with words work on the regulation of intense affective states (perhaps because no one has modeled this effectively for him).

How does co-regulation fit into the cognitive triad of CBT?

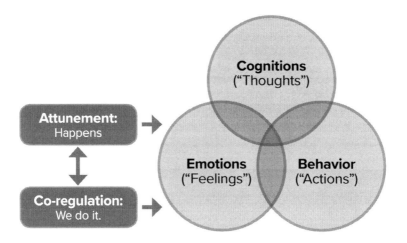

Figure 11

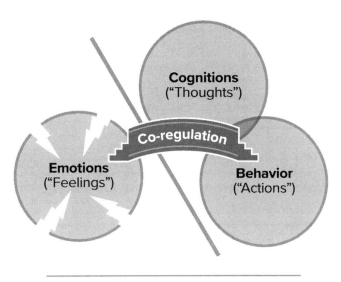

Emotions are intense. Client can't reflect.
Client is stuck "feeling" and can't do anything
else. Co-regulation can bridge the gap between
client feelings and thoughts and actions.

Figure 12

Co-regulation builds the bridge from the emotional component to the cognitive and behavioral components of the cognitive triad. When your client is stuck in an emotional state, unable to reflect on it in any way, co-regulation helps your client build a connection: It moves the emotional part of the cognitive triad back into the triad. You can now do CBT instead of being stuck in the emotional component of the work. You could also say that co-regulation gets your client ready to do CBT. A client in a regulated and balanced affective state can better think, reflect, and act.

Ultimately the experience of co-regulation is meant to implicitly teach self-regulation. If your client already self regulates well, co-regulation is not really needed. Attunement, however, will and should continue.

Client can now connect and reflect.

Figure 13

Just like attunement, co-regulation is used in the service of accessing the full cognitive triad with your client.

A word on co-regulation and posttraumatic stress disorder:

Before you can help a client regulate his or her state of mind using co-regulation, you have to be willing and able to attune to the client's state of mind. Feeling someone else's despair and hopelessness is no easy task. The key is to feel with the client, to be with the client, but not to make his state of mind and feelings your own.

You are not taking on the client's trauma-based state of mind, thinking and feeling, but you are getting to know it so that you can then help your client regulate. Interestingly, if you are attuned with your client and you are helping him co-regulate, he is no longer alone. This in itself can help lift the intense feelings of loneliness and despair.

You will also need to be prepared to bear witness to feelings of intense anger and rage. It may be tempting to immediately "talk your client out of" feelings of rage. Keep in mind that before you can help your client make changes in the way he feels, you need to attune and be a witness. This, of course, is not the same as endorsing violent behavior. You are simply communicating that you can "hold" your client's intense emotions.

Remember the steps:
1.   attunement, implicit acknowledgment and acceptance of what is
2.   co-regulation
3.   self-regulation

CBT Techniques and CBT Structure

Sometimes CBT can seem a bit formulaic to a therapist. This can happen when you think of CBT as a set of rules and techniques. You may think that you have to use an automatic thought record if you are doing CBT with a client. Or you may rigidly stick to an established structure for a session when what is needed is flexibility and attunement.

Tolin (2016) used the analogy of being a chef verses being a cook (p. 9).

When you are doing CBT: Be a chef. Add your own flavor. Serve what the client is likely going to eat. But also serve something that stretches the client's palate. This is how your client grows.

You can use many techniques within CBT as long as this is done within the context of the foundation of CBT—in other words, as long as you are working with your client on changing cognitions, emotions, and behavior to better fit the reality he or she is facing.

What About CBT Techniques and Structure when Treating PTSD?

Trauma can create all kinds of chaos in the life of a trauma survivor. Creating a structure, as CBT does, can be very helpful. But be flexible and adapt to the challenges that trauma presents to you in treatment. Think back to the amoeba model of treatment. While it is good to have a structure for every session, you may have to veer from the structure if your client is triggered into a dissociative episode. Clearly, when your client is dissociative, you can't work on examining faulty cognitions.

Understand that it is not helpful for your client if you label faulty cognitions that are trauma based as such. Calling thoughts "faulty" can imply that your client is doing something wrong. Accept and understand that trauma-based cognitions were likely adaptive and protective at some point in time. In other words, they made sense then, but they have become unhelpful now.

You can adapt classic CBT by using ACT (acceptance and commitment therapy) terminology (Harris, 2009). Ask:

- *Is this a workable story?*

- *Are these helpful thoughts/feelings/behaviors?*

- *Do these thoughts/feelings/behaviors move you in the direction of a life based on your values?*

There are many ways in which CBT is different from other forms of therapy. CBT is more directive and more structured than other forms of treatment for PTSD. Treatment has a structure. There are things to be learned. Every session has a structure. You can step away from the structure of the session. You can be flexible, but you still need a plan. To continue the culinary analogy: There is a menu. The menu can vary, but there is always a menu. For the treatment of PTSD, this makes sense: PTSD can make your clients seem aimless. They may have no structure in their days and no plan how to move forward because they are still immersed and stuck in a trauma-driven way of being.

CBT creates a structure and a plan for your client. The message to your client is: There is a way to get better. I can help you move forward step by step.

Creating Structure

Treatment has a structure. As Tolin (2016) put it: "CBT tends to not be a forever, Woody Allen–style treatment" (p. 8).

Treatment is focused on the collaboratively established goals, not on other things that come up in the course of treatment/the course of a session. This does not mean that treatment goals can't be revised. If a client develops suicidal ideation, clearly the treatment plan needs to be revisited and revised.

Is there a prescribed length of treatment?

As client problems vary, so does length of treatment. Dobson & Dobson (2017) referenced a 12–16 session length (p. 95). But this length refers to length of treatment in treatment studies. There is no one answer to the question of duration. Here is a rough guideline:

- If your client has experienced a single-incident, adult-onset trauma, has no other mental health challenges (such as addiction/depression/anxiety) and no significant therapy-interfering conditions (such as the lifelong experience of toxic stress), treatment duration may be in the 16–20 session range.

- If your client has suffered from developmental and complex trauma and/or toxic stress, treatment will most likely need to last longer. There are many reasons for this, one of them being that it may take longer to establish a therapeutic alliance due to the client's experience of relational betrayals. A treatment duration of 24–32 sessions is reasonable. Extending treatment beyond this range is also reasonable if your client's lack of capacity to regulate emotions and relate to others significantly impairs functioning. Complex trauma often requires complex treatment. You should use all appropriate and available treatment modalities and wrap services around your client to support recovery.

    ○ Here is an example: Your adult client suffered extensive abuse as a child and spent several years in foster homes and treatment facilities. As a result, your client has developed a disorganized attachment style that has carried over into adult relationships. The first few meetings with your client are chaotic. Your client has multiple anger outbursts and alternately looks for you to tell him what to do and then accuses you of trying to control him. Your client is unemployed and has lost several jobs due to his inability to manage relationships and emotions. Your client often feels overwhelmed, shuts down in sessions, and needs assistance with being present in the here and now. In this scenario, relationships and skill building are likely going to be complex and will require additional time.

- Other mental health challenges such as addictions, depression, anxiety, or other mood and psychotic disorders complicate treatment. Again, a treatment duration of 24–32 sessions is reasonable. Treatment for co-occurring conditions should be concurrent and integrated. Use all appropriate and available treatment modalities, and wrap services around your client to support recovery.

    ○ Here is an example: Your client has been become hopeless and helpless. Her PTSD is now complicated by an episode of major depression that is not responding to psychological treatment. You should quickly recommend a psychiatry referral and other supportive services, such as TBS. Depression is likely impacting your client's capacity to think clearly. If your client cannot think clearly, she cannot engage in reflection about her thoughts.

Community Mental Health Practice Alert

Clients in a community mental health setting often present with a multiplicity of symptoms and problems. Our clients are often dually diagnosed and physically ill. They may have depression and PTSD. They may have lifelong exposure to toxic stress. At OhioGuidestone, more than 55% of our clients have an ACE score of 4 or more, putting them at a much higher risk for a variety of physical and mental health problems. What this means is that your client may have depression and diabetes, or depression and heart disease. They may also struggle with an addiction, often undiagnosed.

If your client struggles with more than one mental health problem and additional physical and environmental problems, it unlikely that treatment duration will fall within the 16–20 week range.

It is important, however, to keep in mind and to discuss with your client that treatment has a beginning and an end. The goal of treatment is to resolve the mental health issues, and you and your client should be aware of where you are in the treatment. Are you just beginning? Are you in the midst of it? Or are you almost done? You and your client should frequently discuss this.

Structure is important. If your client feels that he has so many problems he may never be done with treatment, this could contribute to a sense of hopelessness. When using CBT, length of treatment can vary depending on the complexity of symptoms and problems. Structure, however, is a constant.

Creating Structure when Discussing Course and Length of Treatment

You can use a simple visual aid like this to discuss the course and possible length of treatment with your client. You can also use this image to assess treatment progress.

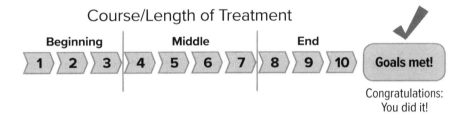

Figure 14

Creating Structure for Each Session

Here is an example of how you can structure a session with your client:

CBT Session Structure

1. **Check-in:** This is brief, perhaps five minutes. Is there anything new that is relevant to treatment? Have symptoms decreased, increased, or remained the same?
2. **Introduce today's task:** Again, this is brief. Identify what needs to be done today. Be collaborative about this. If your client is unfocused and wants to add things that are not relevant to treatment, it is OK to refer to treatment goals. If new things have come up, help the client evaluate how they fit into treatment and rate how important it is to address them right now. Will they detour treatment or move the client forward?

3. **Homework review:** Homework is an integral component of CBT. Homework brings the content of therapy into the real world. This is where skills will need to be practiced, and new ways of thinking/doing/feeling will be tried. Celebrate successes, even the small ones, and problem-solve about things that did not work.

4. **Work on today's task:** This is where the "meat" of your session takes place. Be sure to anchor your work in the treatment plan and the cognitive triad. This is where your behavioral, emotional, or cognitive work takes place.

5. **Summarize the work:** You are the guide through treatment and through each session. Summarize periodically what you are talking about and how this fits into treatment progress.

6. **Identify new homework:** New homework can originate from the homework review at the beginning of the session and/or today's tasks. You and the client can identify what needs practice. Be sure that homework can realistically be accomplished.

7. **Closing:** Summarize session takeaways. Clarify questions. Provide feedback about session.

Adapted from Persons, Davidson, and Tompkins, Essential Components of Cognitive Behavioral Therapy for Depression, APA, Washington, DC, 2001.

Here is a simplified version to keep handy for your client as you travel through each session:

CBT Session Structure
Check-In
Identify Today's Task
Homework Review
Work on Today's Task
Summarize the Work
Identify New Homework
Closing

Figure 15

Keep in mind that your PTSD client may be triggered into a trauma-related state while in session and that you will need to veer from the established structure when this happens. Add a "grounding" component to each session that can be "picked up" as needed.

Essential CBT Techniques

Remember, CBT can borrow techniques from a variety of evidence-based forms of therapy such as dialectical behavior therapy or acceptance and commitment therapy. There are, however, a few essential intervention components you should use.

Psychoeducation

Dobson and Dobson (2017) defined psychoeducation "as the provision of information about relevant psychological principles and knowledge" (p. 96).

Psychoeducation takes place throughout the course of treatment. At the beginning of treatment, you should provide the client with appropriate information about:

- PTSD: Symptoms and treatment

- CBT 101: Go over the cognitive triad (but don't call it that). It is important that your client understands that he will be working on thoughts, feelings, and behaviors, and that these are connected. You can also determine together where the client is most willing and able to start work. For many of our clients, behavioral work is the most accessible work.

- The nature of CBT. Explain that CBT is collaborative, structured, focused, and present-oriented. If your client suffers from PTSD, you should also explain that being present-oriented includes recognizing the pain that trauma has caused but focusing on improving life in the present. CBT recognizes and honors this pain by helping your client recover from the trauma and build a full life. This does not mean that the trauma will be gone; rather, that the trauma will be in the past and not occupy the present.

- Skill building: Explain that skills for managing symptoms can be learned. This information in itself can give hope.

- Resources: Periodically assess what your client needs. Does he need access to an advocacy or support group? Legal assistance? Job training? Resource building is an important aspect of CBT because increased access to resources gives your client an opportunity to act. As PTSD can lead to complete helplessness and hopelessness, helping your client build a roadmap for action can be life-changing.

Socratic Questioning

Socratic questioning is a process of asking open-ended questions that point your client toward alternative and more realistic ways of thinking. Socratic questions point in the direction of evidence. It is up to your client to discover the answers to your Socratic questions and the impact that the newly discovered evidence can have on thinking, feelings, and being. Remember, telling your client the answers to the questions you are asking is not effective. The experience of trauma often leads to the disappearance of choices. Things have happened to your client. The things that happened were not her/his choice. This is why it is so important that your client now be allowed to examine and make choices. You are asking Socratic questions to help your client recognize that you will not make her/his choices. Psychotherapy should not be something that happens *to* the client, but rather something that is collaboratively done with the client.

Homework

Tolin (2016) identified the following kinds of homework (p. 154):

- **Reading assignments** tailored to the client's specific needs and abilities.
  - o This can be tricky for our clients. Keep in mind that many of our adult clients read on a third- to fifth-grade level. Assess your client's ability to take in written information. Keep it simple. Use handouts that contain visual representations of the information you want your client to review. Reading assignments are a form of psychoeducation. They are also designed to empower and change the way your client thinks about himself, others, and the world.
  - o Also keep in mind that your client with PTSD may have difficulty taking in information. Your client may have a constant neuroception of danger (Porges, 2011), leaving little mental energy for learning. Written information should be short and simple, in addition to being appropriate to your client's reading level.

- **Self-monitoring**
  - o You can create simple checklists to help your client monitor problematic behaviors and thoughts. Be sure to explain that self-monitoring is designed to establish a baseline and determine treatment needs. Here is what a simple monitoring chart could look like:

	Mon	Tue	Wed	Thu	Fri	Sat	Sun
Hours in bed							
Hours of TV							

Figure 16

- You can use this chart over the course of several weeks to monitor decreased time spent in bed (if this is a goal). Honesty, of course, is key to self-monitoring. Be sure that you collaborate with your client on a realistic goal and a charting system that feels right.

- Clients with PTSD may use self-monitoring charts as a way to be judgmental about themselves. When this happens, introduce the concept of self-compassion (Neff, 2011).

Learning and Practicing New Behaviors

Skills Training

- New skills will have to be learned together in session, then practiced in the real world. Explain to your client that there is no such thing as failure when practicing a new skill or behavior. Each "mistake" will guide both of you to refine the work, examine negative automatic thoughts, and present new learning opportunities. Enthusiastically welcome each perceived mistake and greet it as a chance to practice self-compassion and learn new ways of thinking, feeling, and doing.

Behavior Changes

- Your client may need specific behavior changes related to PTSD symptoms that lead to feelings of helplessness, hopelessness, disconnect, and rage. Collaboratively pick a behavior your client wants to change. Clearly map out the new behavior in session. It is a good idea to use a self-monitoring chart to track the new behavior. Be sure to keep it simple and set realistic goals. Instead of asking your client to visit a family member/friend every day, ask your client to contact a family member/friend three times a week. Identify who your client will contact and verify the phone number or address. Here is a simple chart to monitor this behavior change:

	Mon	Tue	Wed	Thu	Fri	Sat	Sun
Contacted friend/ family member X							

Figure 17

- By setting a realistic goal, you are increasing the likelihood that your client can be successful. Celebrate the small successes, then raise the bar. Move from the task of contacting a person to spending time with that person.

- If your client is truly isolated, this is an important clinical issue by itself. Go back to resource building. Brainstorm with your client. Find a support/advocacy group. Connect your client with peer supports. All of this creates a path to action.

Behavioral Activation

There are many messages your client receives from PTSD symptoms. Here are a few examples:

- "This is hopeless."
- "Nothing I do matters."
- "People are just out to hurt each other."
- "I need to stay home to stay safe."
- "Life is pain."
- "It's all my fault."

These messages contain a variety of cognitive errors that lead to behavior changes that are not helpful, such as:

- not doing anything meaningful;
- giving up;
- not trusting anyone;
- staying home all the time; perhaps losing a job;
- ineffective self-soothing, such as eating too much, substance abuse, etc.; and
- inaction.

A vicious cycle of symptoms ensues:

Figure 18

Provide psychoeducation to your client about this cycle. Explain that just by changing one part, the whole cycle can begin to change. Express understanding that changing trauma-based thoughts and feelings can be hard and suggest that you start by changing behaviors, by scheduling activities and altering the environment.

Explain that it is OK if activities are not fun at first and that, over time, with practice, enjoyment will return.

Here is what the cycle of behavioral change will look like:

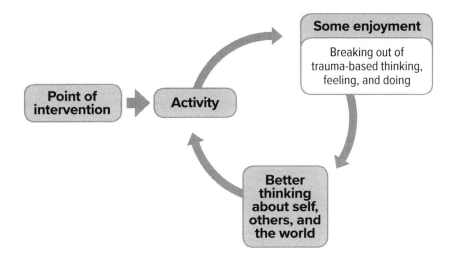

Figure 19

Tolin (2016) outlined the benefits of activity scheduling and explains that it goes hand in hand with self-monitoring (pp. 224–226). While it is good to be ambitious about behavioral changes and activity scheduling, it is equally important to be realistic. You are teaching your client to create achievable behavioral goals.

Here is a simple activity schedule you can use with clients. The further you are in treatment, the more meaningful activities you may want to schedule.

	Morning	Afternoon	Evening
Mon			
Tue			
Wed			
Thu			
Fri			
Sat			
Sun			

Figure 20

Cognitive Restructuring

Let's take another look at the role of thoughts/cognitions in CBT.

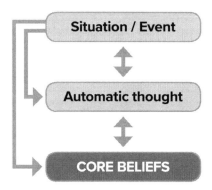

Figure 21: Note that core beliefs are much harder to identify than automatic thoughts. ATs just appear; we do not have to ask for them. Because they appear so often, they are easier to bring into conscious awareness.

Negative and trauma-based core beliefs are partially at the root of PTSD symptoms. But those core beliefs can be difficult to uncover. They are triggered by a situation or event. Once a core belief is triggered, it sends out its "messengers"—those pesky negative automatic thoughts.

And when you have PTSD, almost anything can trigger negative and trauma-based automatic thoughts and feelings, and even trauma-based states of body and mind. The trigger may no longer be directly related to the traumatic event. Your client may once have been triggered by thinking about her ex-partner who attempted to kill her, but she is now triggered into a trauma state any time she sees a male. It is important to think of this "trigger-extension" as an attempt to be self-protective.

Negative automatic thoughts are much easier to address because they show up all the time and they may even bug your client. Here are some examples of automatic thoughts:

- "I always mess everything up."

- "She hates me."

- "I am going to fail this one."

Automatic thoughts can be examined. In CBT you and your client are looking for evidence for and against the truth of the automatic thought.

Here is what this would look like:

A situation or event triggers a negative automatic thought, which in turn will affect the way your client feels. But what if the thought was just a thought, like the brain letting off some steam? We should examine thoughts and ask: Is this a realistic thought? Or is this just my brain blowing off some steam? (You could also use the term *brain fart*.)

Automatic Thought	Evidence for AT	Evidence against AT
It's my fault.	I went to his house. (Be sure to examine if this is really evidence for the AT; it probably is not, but just seems like it).	I took my cell phone with me. He took violent action. I attempted to protect myself by . . . . . .
She hates me.	She is mad at me about the thing I said.	We have been dating for 6 months. We make each other laugh. She called me to talk. . . .
I am failing.	Failed spelling test.	Just got into district art show. Passing grades, even in spelling. . . .

Figure 22 (A blank version can be found in the appendix.)

Keep in mind that automatic thoughts can be relentless. Once you have examined them with your client, it is OK to use humor when one shows up. You can talk to an automatic thought! Here is an example:

> *Hello there. You are trying to trick me. Not going to happen. You, my uninvited friend, are just a brain fart. Stinky and unpleasant. I am going to leave you now and think better thoughts. Goodbye!*

If your client presents with a trauma-related automatic thought, you may want to say something like:

> *Hello. There you are again. You have protected me in the past, but now that I am safe, I no longer need you, and I no longer believe you. It's OK for you to stop by sometimes. You remind me of tough times that are in the past. It's OK for me to think about the past. But I don't want to live in it.*

Talking to the automatic thought in this way creates distance, it defuses, and it is far easier to examine a faulty thought from a distance (Harris, 2009)!

Why do you want your client to examine automatic thoughts?

Because automatic thoughts create feelings based on these faulty automatic thoughts. If your client can dismiss those automatic thoughts, then he can begin to let go of the feelings based on them.

If you and your client run into a set of automatic thoughts with a similar theme, you are probably on to a core belief. Core beliefs, too, can be examined for their truthfulness.

CBT Interventions for PTSD

Adapting the Stage-Model of PTSD Treatment

Interventions for the treatment of PTSD will be presented sequentially. Please keep in mind that PTSD symptoms can wax and wane and that you will need to respond to your client's needs. The amoeba model of PTSD treatment requires you to have an awareness of where the client is and what your client needs.

Don't think of stages of treatment as "done." You may have to revisit them as your client's needs change, and this is perfectly OK. You are moving through and among the stages of treatment.

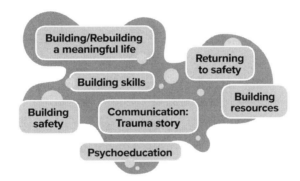

Figure 24

You may want to think of components of treatment as opposed to states of treatment. Remember that while the goal of treatment is to build a better life, this goal is not an "end product." It's important to build a life while in treatment. Meaningful relationships are an important component of life. Build a meaningful relationship with your client, perhaps one that can serve as a model for other relationships. Once again, working collaboratively is of the essence.

The following image shows the treatment components:

Figure 25

Building Safety

When working with traumatized clients, safety can be an issue in many different ways. Here are a few examples:

- Your client's traumatic experience has been so painful that she is suicidal.
- You client stays indoors to avoid any danger.
- You client uses drugs/alcohol to soothe the pain.
- You client enters violent relationships.
- Your client seeks high-intensity situations that are inherently dangerous.
- Your client engages in unsafe sex.
- Your client is violent with others.
- Your client wants to hurt/kill the person that hurt him.
- Your client is full of shame and feels unworthy or undeserving, perhaps in a spiritual way.

Building safety means breaking away from neurobiological states of hyperarousal that may have become normal for your client. Your client wants to feel and be safe, but her central nervous system is on constant alert, looking for danger. This hyper-aroused state of mind and body cannot simply be turned off. It has become baseline, and your client needs a baseline re-set. This will take time and practice.

The following interventions are designed to help your client build safety over time by thinking and acting differently. If your client is in an acute crisis, refer to the safety planning section of this manual.

Using the Instructions

All interventions noted below contain detailed instructions. Most of the time instructions will tell you what you may want to say, but you should feel free to adjust the exact wording to fit your style and the client's situation and vocabulary. Sometimes it is important to use the exact words outlined in the intervention. When this is the case, the wording will be in quotation marks.

Building Safety Interventions

INTERVENTION 1

Safety Is a Place You Build

This intervention asks your client to create a protected space, one that she can relax in. The intervention is suited for children and adults. Simply adjust materials and methods as needed.

Target skill: Recognizing and building safe spaces.

What you will need: Building materials like cardboard, glue, Legos, or drawing paper and pencils. You could even knit a safe space or use pillows and blankets in your office.

1. Begin with empathy. Welcome your client. Check in about the past week. Ask questions like:

   - *What went well?*

   - *What did you enjoy?*

   - *What did not go well?*

   - *What were you afraid of?*

   - *Did you get hurt in the past week?*

   - *Did anyone hurt you? Did you hurt yourself?*

   If your client is a risk to self or others, move into safety planning.

   Listen compassionately. Learn as much as you can about your client's sense of safety and how this may relate to the traumatic experience. Listen for a longing to be safe.

2. Introduce today's task: recognizing and building safe spaces. You can say:

   - *It sounds to me like you really want a space where you can just be, and you do not have to worry about getting hurt or hurting yourself.*

   Suggest that such a space can be built. With an adult, you can explain that it can be helpful to envision the space and create a replica of it as a reminder.

   If your client struggles with the thought that there can be safe spaces in the world, accept this as her experience. Value her experience. But throw in the idea that just because her experience has told her that there are no safe spaces does not mean that safe spaces do not exist or cannot be built.

3. Work on today's task: Ask your client to build or draw a space in which she would feel safe. If your client needs inspiration, ask questions like:

   - *Is it a house, or is it a tower?*

   - *Is the safe space underground, or is it in a tree?*

   - *Is it a large space or a small space?*

   - *What is in the space?*

   - *Who is there with you?*

It may be helpful to talk about a safe house, but emphasize that the house can have many shapes or forms.

4. While your client is drawing or building, you may want to assist by handing materials to her. In this manner you are there to show that no one should be alone when they build a safe space. But be sure not to take over. This is your client's safe space. Your ideas may be great, but they are yours.

5. When your client is done, ask: *Does this space need another layer of security? Perhaps a wall with a door, or a dome above it?*

6. Once your client has finished creating the space, ask her to imagine living in it. Ask questions like:

   - *What would it be like?*
   - *What would you do?*
   - *Who would you allow in?*
   - *Would you ever leave if you knew that you could come back any time?*

7. Help your client reflect on safety, or the lack thereof, in her life. Reframe safety as something that trauma has stolen from her but that she can get back. You can say things like:

   - *It's not you.*
   - *This has been taken from you, but you can take it back. You can build it again or anew.*

   (If your client built a space, be sure to ask her to take a picture of it. You will need it for your next meeting.)

8. Summarize what you have done today:

   - You have listened for the desire to be safe.
   - You have explored the idea of a safe space and have created an image or model of a safe space.
   - Your client has explored what she needs to feel safe.

9. Assign homework: Ask your client to pick one element from her drawing or model that would make her feel safe in the real world. Then ask her to use this element in some way in her real life every day. Here are some examples of what might work:

   - Your client uses blankets to feel protected. Ask her to wrap herself gently in a blanket every evening.
   - Your client feels safe when she holds a treasured object, like a stuffed animal. Ask her to hold this object with love at the beginning of every day.
   - Your client feels safe when she talks to her grandmother. Ask her to talk to or write to her grandmother once a day. Remember: This could be an imaginary conversation.

Ask your client to check off the daily safety task on this list. Using a checklist will increase the likelihood that your client will complete the homework.

Daily Safe Space:
Monday:
Tuesday:
Wednesday:
Thursday:
Friday:
Saturday:
Sunday:

Figure 26

10. Closing: Ask about barriers to completing the homework. Ask questions like:

- *What do you think may get in the way of bringing the safe space into your life?*
- *Are there reasons you are reluctant to do this?*

Address barriers before your client leaves. Don't brush them aside. Work with your client to overcome them. These barriers will tell you more about what your client thinks and believes and what her life is like. You can say things like:

- *I am so glad you are telling me about this now.*
- *That sounds complicated/tough.*
- *In what way do you think you can work around that?*

Be prepared to collaborate with your client. What is she able and willing to do?

INTERVENTION 2

Moving Toward Safety

This intervention asks your client to rethink the idea that feeling safe or unsafe is something that just "happens." It introduces the idea that safety is something to walk toward. Thoughts and feelings that trigger feelings and behaviors that are unsafe to your client now become a signal to move into safety as opposed to triggering anxiety.

Target skill: Moving into safety. Using a safety plan mindfully. Seeking help.

What you will need: Image of the safe space your client created. Paper. Writing tools.

1. Begin with empathy. Welcome your client. Ask questions like:

    - *How did the last week go?*
    - *When did you feel safe?*
    - *When did you not feel safe?*
    - *When you did not feel safe, do you remember what started that feeling?*

2. **Introduce today's task:** moving toward safety. You can explain by saying:

    - *Safety is not always there. But you can build it.*
    - *It takes practice to build safety.*

3. Review last week's homework. Take a look at your client's Daily Safe Space chart together. Was your client able to complete the chart? Elicit feedback: How did it feel to create this safe space daily? What went well? Listen reflectively for clues as to what your client thinks and does when he feels or becomes unsafe. Reflect back to your client what he does when this happens. You can say:

    - *It sounds to me like this happens when you feel unsafe . . .*
    - *Am I getting this right? When you feel unsafe you . . .*

4. Work on today's task: When you reflect back to your client what he does, begin to shift your language by adding words that indicate action instead of passivity. Here are some things you might want to say:

    - *In what way did you feel powerless?*
    - *In what way did you feel you still had choices to make?*
    - *What ideas did you have about moving toward safety?*
    - *Is there anyone you thought of contacting?*

    Take out the image of a safe space your client has created. If your client built a space (instead of drawing), be sure to have a picture of it ready.

    Ask your client, once more, to recall a moment in which he felt unsafe. Say something like:

    > *You are right there, on the threshold of feeling unsafe and maybe out of control.*

Now, look at the place of safety you created for yourself. You did this. It is your very own space.

I understand that you are having this thought of feeling unsafe. Look at the place you have created for yourself. Now, walk into it.

5. If your client is confused by the idea of walking into an image, just explain by saying something like:

   We are going to use your very own safe space to create the feeling of safety.

   I understand that you can't really walk into a picture. In your mind, though, you can do this. I would like to ask you to try.

   Take another look at the picture of your safe space. Take in every detail. When you have done so, you may want to close your eyes, but you do not have to.

   Now imagine that you are walking into this space. You are walking away from feeling unsafe, and you are walking toward safety. Not anyone else's idea of safety. This space has exactly what you need because you created it.

6. As your client listens, describe the space in detail. Ask if there is anyone who needs to join your client there, or anything that would make the space even better. Then ask your client to add those things to the space in his mind.

7. When you have fully described the space, ask your client to just be in it. There are no demands. There is nothing he has to do. He can simply rest, being completely safe in the space he has created.

8. Ask your client to take a few deep breaths to settle in.

9. Wait for a minute or two. Then ask your client to take another deep breath and open his eyes. Give your client a minute to return back to the space you are occupying. You can say something like, *Welcome back to my office.*

10. Summarize what you have done together: You have explored what triggers your client to feel unsafe. You have introduced the idea that he can move toward safety. You have used your client's image of a safe space to create a refuge in his mind, a space he can always walk into no matter where he is. You have helped your client settle into this space.

11. Ask questions like:

    - *What was this experience like?*

    - *What was helpful? What was not?*

    - *Were there specific moments that gave you a sense of peace and safety? If there were, what were they?*

12. Assign homework: Give your client the image of safety he has created (if it is a picture saved on her phone he already has it). Ask him to set aside 3–5 minutes per day to walk toward safety. Explain that this is something that needs to be practiced every day so that walking toward safety will becomes a habit. It won't be difficult anymore.

13. Give your client the following helpful tracking chart to check off homework completion every day.

Daily Safe Space:
Monday:
Tuesday:
Wednesday:
Thursday:
Friday:
Saturday:
Sunday:

Figure 27

14. Closing: Address barriers before your client leaves. Don't brush them aside. Work with your client to work around them or with them. These barriers will tell you more about what your client thinks and believes and what his life is like. You should say things like:

- *I am so glad you are telling me about this now.*

- *That sounds complicated/tough.*

- *In what way do you think you can work around that?*

Be prepared to collaborate with your client. What is he able and willing to do?

INTERVENTION 3

Choosing Connection

This intervention expands the idea of safe spaces to include the idea of people who can provide safe connection and co-create safety with your client. When safety is in question, there is almost always disconnection from others. Truly meaningful connections create safety. They acknowledge pain but also celebrate meaning through interaction. Neurobiologically speaking, humans are meant to be with each other. Meaningful connection can help regulate difficult states of mind.

Target skill: Connection seeking. Creating joy.

What you will need: Paper. Writing tools. Colored pencils/crayons.

1. Welcome your client and begin with empathy. Ask questions like:

   - *How was the last week?*

   - *Who did you talk to?*

   - *Who did you see?*

   - *When did you feel safe?*

   - *When did you not feel safe?*

   - *When you did not feel safe, do you remember how that feeling started?*

2. **Introduce today's task:** finding ways to connect with others to create safety and joy.

3. Review last week's homework. Take a look at the Daily Safe Space tracking chart. Was your client able to complete the assignment every day? If she did: What went well? What was difficult? If she was not able to complete the assignment: What were the barriers? Does the assignment need tweaking? If your client was able to complete the assignment some of the time, collaborate on realistic expectations. Perhaps five out of seven days is a realistic goal. You want her to succeed.

4. Work on today's task: choosing connection. Provide psychoeducation about the healing powers of meaningful connection with others. You may want to say the following things:

   - *Humans are made to be with each other. Being alone is not how we are meant to be.*

   - *Being alone (when you don't want to be) can increase emotional distress.*

   - *Being with a caring person (when feeling unsafe) can decrease emotional distress.*

   - *Healing takes place within caring relationships.*

   - *Caring relationships can be chosen and built.*

5. Ask your client about the people in her life that make her feel safe and connected. If you are working with a child, you may also want to ask your client to draw this person.

6. If your client can't identify a person, ask about pets. Pets, too, provide con-nection, and they do it without explanation and ask little in return. If you are working with a child, ask your client to draw a picture of the pet.

7. Sometimes important people are not there, meaning that they live far away or are deceased. If your client can't name a living person or a pet, but they can name a deceased person such as a grandmother, that's OK. However:

   • Be sure that your client does not glamorize the person *because* they are deceased. Instead ask about the positive feelings this person elicited. Pay attention to affect. If you see your client's face softening when she talks about this person, say so. In this way you are bringing this person into the room and into the present.

   • Stay in the present. Help your client elicit feelings of connection and support in the here and now. Ask what dreams the person had for your client and focus on affirming life here and now, with that person in mind.

   • If there is sadness, acknowledge it. Say: "Your sadness shows how deeply connected you are with this person. You are capable of love and you are loved."

8. It's also OK to think about an imaginary important person in your client's life. If a child client feels a special connection with the hero of a children's movie, you can ask about this in the following way:

   • *In what way do you feel connected with or close to* [imaginary important person in client's life]*?*

   • *How do you feel when you think about* [imaginary important person in client's life]*?*

   • *What do you think* [imaginary important person in client's life] *would say to you right now?*

9. Once your client has chosen a person or character, be sure to bring this person into the room by asking as many questions about this person as you can. All of your questions should point in the direction of safety, support, and connection. Here are a few sample questions:

   • *What is it about this person that makes you feel safe?*

   • *Can you describe how you feel when you see this person?*

   • *Can you describe how you feel when you hear this person's voice?*

   • *What do you do when you are together?*

   • *How do you feel when you are together?*

   • *Can you describe this person's face? What does he or she look like?*

   • *For a moment, could you look at me like this person looks at you?*

10. Ask your client to create an image that stands for the presence of this person. If your client has a photo, that's great. If you are working with a child, have

the child draw either this person in as much detail as possible or an object that reminds them of this person.

11. The image should elicit a strong emotional reaction in your client, specifically, feelings of safety and connection.

12. Laminate the image/picture. If you do not have a laminator, you can simply use tape. It's just a bit more work.

13. Ask your client to carry the image with her all the time.

14. Instruct your client to take out the image right now and look at it with love.

15. Pay attention to your client's facial expression. If you see your client's face softening, say so. Bring the feelings of safety and connection into the room.

16. Summarize what you have done together today. Your client has learned about the importance and healing power of connection with others (person or pet). She has also identified a person she feels connected with and has created a reminder image of this person to carry with her.

17. Assign homework: Ask your client to carry the image of the chosen person or pet with her and schedule a daily time to look at the image with love. Once again, give your client the following chart to increase probability of homework completion.

Spending time with my person/pet:
Monday:
Tuesday:
Wednesday:
Thursday:
Friday:
Saturday:
Sunday:

Figure 28

18. Additionally, ask your client to take out the image when she is feeling unsafe, look at the image with love, and consciously choose to connect with the person/pet in the image.

19. Closing: Address barriers before your client leaves. Don't brush them aside. Work with your client to address potential barriers. These barriers will tell

you more about what your client thinks and believes and what her life is like. You can say things like:

- *I am so glad you are telling me about this now.*

- *That sounds complicated/tough.*

- *In what way do you think you can work around that?*

Be prepared to collaborate with your client. What is she able and willing to do?

INTERVENTION 4

That's Quite a Thought

This intervention asks your client to gain some distance from their thoughts of harm. The idea is to get your client to understand that all thoughts can be examined, even thoughts of harm. There is no need to simply believe the thought and run with it or fear it. You will ask your client to *defuse* or step away from the thought. Once your client is no longer fused with the thought, it has lost its power. It is present but no longer a threat.

Target skill: Defusing from thoughts of self-harm and harm to others. Mindful acceptance of thoughts and feelings.

What you will need: Paper. Writing tools.

1. Welcome your client and begin with empathy. Ask questions like:

    - *How was the last week?*

    - *Who did you talk to?*

    - *Who did you see?*

    - *When did you feel safe?*

    - *When did you not feel safe?*

    - *When you did not feel safe, do you remember how that feeling started?*

    - *What did you do in response to not feeling safe? Did you use your safe space or your safe person?*

2. **Introduce today's task:** gaining distance from thoughts of self-harm.

3. Review last week's homework: Take a look at your client's My Person/Pet homework chart. Did your client complete the homework? If he did, ask her about a day when this really made a difference for him. If he did not, ask what got in the way. Be specific. Ask about barriers such as lack of time or emotional reluctance. Help your client identify ways of overcoming those barriers. It's OK to reduce the frequency of the task if this helps increase the likelihood of homework completion, but remember: The goal is to help your client develop a habit of visiting his safe space/person. The habit won't develop if he only does this very occasionally. It's best not to go under five out of seven days.

4. Work on today's task. You can say something like:

    - *I have noticed that sometimes when you have a thought of self-harm, that thought kind of takes over.*

    - *Tell me more about how thoughts of self-harm tend to take over your thinking.*

    - *I am wondering if there is a way to take power away from those thoughts.*

5. Introduce the idea that a thought is just a thought. You can say things like:

    - *A thought is not a thing.*

    - *Thoughts don't always matter.*

- *Thoughts come and go.*
- *It's possible to think things that seem contradictory.*
- *Thoughts don't automatically have power.*
- *It's possible to gain distance from thoughts of self-harm.*

6. Invite your client to examine a thought together with you. Ask your client to name a repetitive and bothersome thought and write it on a piece of paper.

7. Because this can be stressful, be sure to help your client regulate his feelings by prompting him to use calm breathing as needed. Here is a simple way to teach your client calm breathing:

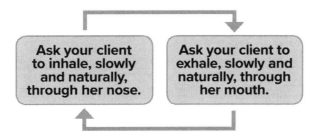

Figure 29

- Demonstrate this at least three times, then practice together.
- Explain that the key for this exercise is to slow down breathing, as fast and shallow breathing can contribute to anxious states.
- You can use the following metaphor to practice: First, smell the soup, then when breathing out, blow on the soup slowly.
- Help your client be nonjudgmental about his breathing. It's OK not to be perfect.

8. Return to the paper containing the thought of self-harm. Ask your client to fold the paper and put it on the table, then help him examine if and how his relationship to the thought has changed, asking the following kinds of questions:

- *How do you feel differently about the thought now that it is on paper and folded up?*
- *How do you feel about putting the thought on paper?*
- *How do you feel about folding up the paper and putting it on the table?*

9. Ask your client to take another look at the paper, unfold it, and read the thought to you. You can say things like:

- *You can pick up this thought, or you can leave it.*
- *You can share this thought with me.*
- *You can put it away again.*

- *You can have a relationship with this thought, but it does not have to dominate you.*

- *It is just a thought.*

10. It's quite possible that your client will say something like: "But the thought is still there. This is stupid. Even when I fold it up and put it away, it is still there."

    You can respond by saying things like:

    - *You are absolutely right. The thought is still there.*

    - *You can relate to this thought by greeting it.*

    - *You can even welcome it.*

    - *No need to push it away. You know from experience that that won't work anyway.*

    - *Once you have greeted it, you can also let it go.*

    - *It does not have to be important today.*

    - *Once you have let it go, the thought might return. Greet it again. Do not argue with it. And let it go again.*

    Return to helping your client understand that a thought is just a thought. He does not have to give it power. You can say things like:

    - *I understand that this is a new way of thinking for you.*

    - *You are thinking about your thoughts.*

    - *You are stepping away from your thoughts to examine them.*

    - *Practicing this will take some time.*

11. Summarize what you have done so far: You have explored the nature of thoughts. Your client has shared a thought of self-harm, and you have explored different ways your client can relate to this thought. You have introduced the idea that thoughts don't have to have power. You explored how to greet a thought and then let it go.

12. Get feedback from your client: How does he feel about this new way of relating to thoughts of self-harm?

13. Assign homework: Ask your client to practice greeting and letting go of thoughts of self-harm using the following script:

    Hello there.
    You are such a tough thought to have.
    And here you are again.
    I did not ask for you to visit, but here you are.
    You are here for a moment.
    But you can go now.
    I am moving on to another thought.
    I let you go.

14. If needed, alter the script together so that it fits your client. Then glue it on an index card and give it to your client to carry. Ask him to use this script every time thoughts of self-harm appear.

15. Closing: If your client finds that he is still bothered by the thought and that it feels like it is gaining power, he can move on to other ways of gaining safety, such as using his safe space and safe person/pet. You can explain that visiting the safe space is another way of not giving the thought power.

INTERVENTION 5

Being of Service

Being of service to someone else is a great way to manage thoughts of self-harm. When we help others, our bodies generate powerful hormones that positively affect how we feel. Being of service does not eliminate or get rid of unwanted thoughts of self-harm, but it can assign them less importance.

Target skill: Embodied empathy. Compassion.

What you will need: It's good to have a list of local organizations that accept volunteers. Look for volunteer opportunities that involve helping a specific person or being as opposed to aiding in a task such as shredding documents. If your client is under the age of 18, organizations often require a parent or guardian to be present when volunteering. If it is difficult to identify an opportunity for your client who is a minor, think outside the box: Check with the parent. Is there an elderly neighbor who needs help? Can your client read to a younger child at school?

1. Welcome your client and begin with empathy. Ask questions like:

   - *How was the last week?*

   - *Who did you talk to?*

   - *Who did you see?*

   - *When did you feel safe?*

   - *When did you not feel safe?*

   - *When you did not feel safe, do you remember how that feeling started?*

   - *What did you do in response to not feeling safe? Did you use your safe space or your safe person? How did you relate to your unsafe thought?*

2. **Introduce today's task:** looking for and choosing ways to be of service, to help others.

3. Review last week's homework: Inquire if your client has used the script for greeting and letting go of unwanted thoughts of self-harm. If she did, in what way was this script helpful? Would she like to make any changes? If she does, make the changes together now. If your client did not use the script, ask what stood in the way.

   Practice using the script together and encourage your client to move past her internal objections to it. Ask her to just give it a try and consider that her objections may be another way in which thoughts of self-harm are seeking to maintain their power.

4. Work on today's task: Provide psychoeducation about the benefits of being of service. If your client would like to learn more about the health benefits of volunteering, give her the article "Volunteering may be good for body and mind" by Stephanie Watson posted on the Harvard Health Blog at www.health.harvard.edu/blog.

   You can summarize by saying things like:

- *Volunteering can make you feel less lonely and more connected.*

- *Volunteering can help you feel less depressed and anxious.*

- *Volunteering can raise the level of powerful natural feel-good hormones in your body.*

5. Help your client make a plan for being of service to others.

  - First, help her identify causes that are truly important to her. You want her to feel connected with what she does.

  - Once you have identified a cause, find out what your client is able to do. Does she have a car? How easy is it for her to get to places? When does she have time? How often does she think she would like to volunteer?

  - Now, match your client's cause and abilities with a need. Be sure that your client has all the information she needs to make contact and schedule an appointment. Make sure your client has picked at least three volunteer opportunities, as things don't always work out on the first try.

  - Help your client understand and accept that organizations have rules for volunteering, and her first attempt to connect may not be successful.

  - If your client expresses frustration about this, this is a great opportunity to practice affect regulation using the following steps:

    - Give feelings a voice.

    - Put those feelings in perspective.

    - Regulate body response using calm breathing.

    - Use a simple feelings-intensity scale to gauge level of emotional response.

    - Repeat calm breathing exercise as needed until body response is calmer.

  Here is a simple feelings-intensity scale you can use:

Figure 30

6. Make the plan to be of service to others concrete by creating a step-by-step process with your client. Here is a chart you can use:

Volunteer activity:	Date and time to complete:
Call three organizations for information	
Schedule appointments to visit	
Visit organization 1	
Visit organization 2	
Visit organization 3	
Make a choice	
Schedule weekly appointments for volunteering	

Figure 31

Of course, this chart may need some tweaking. If your client is a minor, a parent/guardian will need to be involved in planning.

7. Summarize what you have done so far: Your client has learned about the benefits of volunteering. She has created a plan for selecting a volunteer activity.

8. Assign homework: Find out how much calling/visiting/planning your client can do until your next session. Highlight those sections as homework. Ask your client to bring the chart back to your next meeting.

9. Closing: Leave your client with words of encouragement, like:

- *Being of service really can make a difference in how you feel.*

- *I think you really can make a difference in this world.*

INTERVENTION 6

Moving into the Body: Quiet Presence

This intervention is designed to help clients move out of their heads (perhaps filled with thoughts of self-harm) and into mindful and quiet presence in the body. There are times in which it is no longer helpful to think about difficult thoughts. This intervention addresses the need for behaviorally based body-mind interventions. If there was an easy way to banish thoughts of self-harm simply by thinking, your client would have already done so.

Target skill: Mindful and quiet presence.

What you will need: Comfortable seating—on a cushion on the floor, or in a chair—and quiet relaxation music. YouTube has a music such as "8 Hour Deep Sleep Music," "Peaceful Music," "Relaxing, Meditation Music," and "Sleep Meditation Music" from YellowBrickCinema-Relaxing Music's YouTube page at https://youtu.be/cAJRaKnDdLw.

1. Welcome your client and begin with empathy. Ask questions like:

    - *How was the last week?*

    - *Who did you talk to?*

    - *Who did you see?*

    - *When did you feel safe?*

    - *When did you not feel safe?*

    - *When you did not feel safe, do you remember how that feeling started?*

    - *What did you do to be of service to others?*

2. **Introduce today's task:** being present, mindfully, in the body.

3. Review last week's homework: Look at last week's Volunteer Activity chart together. Was your client able to complete the highlighted activities? If he was, compliment him on a job well done. Find out what your client is able to do in the following week and highlight those areas in a different color. The goal is to get your client into a meaningful volunteer activity within a reasonable amount of time. Some people may be able to start volunteering within a week or so. Many may need more time, perhaps 3–4 weeks.

    If your client was not able to complete the highlighted activities, explore together what got in the way. Identify what can realistically be done in the next week. If your client is not ready to volunteer, return to this intervention once he is further along in treatment.

4. Work on today's task: experiencing mindful and quiet presence with the body. Provide psychoeducation about the powerful interconnectedness of the mind and the body. You can say:

    - *Your body and mind are connected.*

    - *Your mind has the ability to impact your body.*

- *Your body has the ability to impact your mind.*

- *It's easy to not be present with the body.*

- *But it can be powerful to learn to be present with the body.*

- *Mindful presence can be learned.*

5.   Ask your client to engage in an exercise to practice mindful presence with you. Ask your client to sit comfortably either on a cushion on the floor or in his chair. Make sure that his body feels well supported. Have extra cushions ready to support the body as needed. If your client is sitting on the floor but wants to lean against the wall, this is perfectly fine.

6.   If your client is comfortable with this, turn on quiet relaxation music. This should be in the background, not too loud.

7.   Use the following script to help your client be mindfully present with the body:

Simply sit. Breathe naturally and let go of worries about your breath. Your body is supported, and you can breathe calmly and naturally in a way that is comfortable for you.

Rest your hands in a comfortable way, perhaps in your lap, perhaps on the ground.

Feel the ground/chair under you. It's OK to wiggle a bit. The ground/chair supports you. If there are cushions, pay attention to the areas in which the cushions support you. Breathe into those areas. When you breathe out, let go of any tension in those areas.

Slowly move your head in a circle from left to right. Take your time. Breathe calmly and naturally.

Then slowly move your head in a circle from right to left. Take your time. Breathe calmly and naturally.

Take a moment to feel the ground/chair under you. Relax into the ground/ chair. Breathe in and out slowly and let go of any tension in your body as you breathe out.

Slowly raise your shoulders. Then gently relax them. Breathe in and out slowly and let go of any tension in your body as you breathe out.

It you are uncomfortable, simply move and adjust your posture.

Slowly raise your arms in front of the center of your body. Turn your hands so your palms are facing up. Breathe in and out slowly and let go of any tension in your body as you breathe out.

Now, simply sit. Breathe calmly and naturally. Be present with your body and all there is around it.

You are supported. You are present.

Let some time pass, whatever seems to work for your client, then continue.

Now, begin to move your body in any way that is comfortable. Wiggle your toes, stretch your arms, stand up, if you wish. Take a deep breath.

8. Help your client reflect on the experience of being mindfully and quietly present with the body. You can use the following prompts/questions:

    - *Tell me how this felt. What has comfortable? What was not?*

    - *In what way did your state of mind change during this exercise?*

    - *How did you feel toward your body?*

    - *What were your thoughts about the body?*

    - *What part of this exercise was helpful?*

    - *Was there anything that was difficult? Did anything make you laugh?*

9. If your client identifies parts of the exercise as not helpful, explain that changes can be made as needed.

10. If your client finds it difficult to be still, provide psychoeducation: Explain that many trauma survivors find it difficult to sit with mindful stillness at first and that this is due to the body's stress response system being constantly on high alert, scanning surroundings for any sign of danger. Explain that practice makes perfect. Over time, your client will be able to reset the way his body responds to stress.

11. If your client did not mention any intrusions by thoughts of self-harm during the exercise, you should say so: "I am noticing that thoughts of self-harm did not come up during this exercise. Perhaps this is a good way for you to let go of them."

12. If thoughts of self-harm did intrude, ask questions like:

    - *How were you able to let go of them during this exercise, at least momentarily?*

    - *What parts of the exercise do you remember as helpful in spite of the presence of thoughts of self-harm?*

The key, in this case, would be for your client to understand that he can be calmly and mindfully present in the body even when he has thoughts of self-harm. He should simply greet them and then let them go.

13. Summarize what you have done today: Your client has learned to be mindfully and quietly present in the body. He has let himself be comfortable and supported.

14. Assign homework: Ask your client to build moments of quiet presence with the body into every day. Give your client the script outlined above to take home. Explain that this can be done in brief chunks of time, perhaps just two minutes in the morning and two minutes in the evening. The key is to build the ability to be mindfully and quietly present in the body. Give your client the following chart to mark his practice of mindful presence:

	Mindful Presence Practice 1	Mindful Presence Practice 2
Mon		
Tue		
Wed		
Thu		
Fri		
Sat		
Sun		

Figure 32

Remind your client to bring the chart back to your next meeting.

15. Closing: Remind your client that becoming mindfully present with the body is a process. You can say:

- *This takes practice.*
- *It's OK to feel frustration. Just be present with that.*
- *This will get easier over time.*

INTERVENTION 7

Moving into the Body: Joyful Presence

This intervention is designed to help clients move out of their heads (perhaps filled with thoughts of self-harm) and into mindful and joyful presence in the body. There are times in which it is no longer helpful to think about difficult thoughts. This intervention addresses the need for behaviorally based body-mind interventions. If there were an easy way to banish thoughts of self-harm, your client would have already done so.

Target skill: Mindful and joyful presence in the body through motion.

What you will need: Sufficient space to move joyfully. Your client should be able to stretch out her arms fully without touching any obstacles. It may be useful to push tables and chairs to the side of the room. You will need music that has a beat and a melody. What you choose will largely depend on what your client likes. For this intervention, you, too, will need to be comfortable with moving your body.

1. Welcome your client and begin with empathy. Ask questions like:

   - *How was the last week?*

   - *Who did you talk to?*

   - *Who did you see?*

   - *When did you feel safe?*

   - *When did you not feel safe?*

   - *When you did not feel safe, do you remember how that feeling started?*

   - *What did you do to be of service to others?*

2. **Introduce today's task:** joyful presence with the body.

3. Review last week's homework: Take a look at your client's Mindful Presence chart. Was she able to build into her day moments of mindful and quiet presence using the script you provided? How often? In what way did this affect her state of mind? What did she find helpful? How did the practice of mindful and quiet presence impact her thoughts of self-harm? In what way did her relationship with those thoughts change?

   If your client was not able to complete the homework most of the time, what got in the way? Work with your client on eliminating barriers. You may have to negotiate frequency. Perhaps your client is only able to schedule one mindful and quiet moment of presence in the body per day, and perhaps only for five out of seven days. This is OK. The key is to schedule enough practice that mindful presence will become a habit.

4. Work on today's task: mindful and joyful presence in the body. Provide psychoeducation. You can say:

   - *Your body and mind are connected.*

   - *Your mind has the ability to impact your body, and your body has the ability to impact your mind.*

- *It's easy to not be present with the body.*

- *Trauma can "settle" in the body.*

- *It can be powerful to learn to be present with the body.*

- *It can be powerful to experience joy through and in the body.*

- *Joyful presence in the body can be learned.*

5. You may want to explain further that trauma can keep your body in survival mode, even after traumatic events have ended. When in survival mode, it can be difficult to experience joy through the body. Perhaps the body often hurts. Perhaps memories of the trauma are stuck. Experiencing joy in the body can be powerful and healing.

6. Ask your client to engage in the following exercise with you:

   - Your client gets to pick a piece of music. She should choose a piece that has a beat and a melody, something she can imagine herself moving to or dancing to. You should be able to access this music on your smart-phone.

   - The music should be joyful and so should the words. Steer your client away from music that glorifies violence in any way. While profanity can provide some temporary relief for the very angry client, this intervention is about joy. If your client is a minor, pay even more attention to the lyrics!

   - Explain that you will both dance/move, but not together. There can be no touching. Body boundaries can be difficult for survivors of sexual trauma. It is your responsibility to establish and maintain appropriate boundaries in therapy.

   - Turn on the music. Explain to your client that she can move slow or fast, and she can move only her arms or her whole body. Explain that you will talk to each other through motion. She gets to start; you will then copy the motion. Then you move and she copies and so forth.

   - Inevitably, there will be some shyness and some laughter. Welcome both.

   - If dancing/moving is very difficult, create a sequence of "oversize" dance moves together, moves so silly that both of you will laugh.

   - For obvious reasons, moves cannot be suggestive and sexualized.

   - If you are working with a child, you can suggest that you each create moves for a specific animal. You could dance like an elephant, and your client can dance like a chicken.

7. When you are done, help your client reflect on the experience. You can use the following prompts/questions:

   - *Tell me how this felt. What was comfortable? What was not?*

   - *In what way did your state of mind change during this exercise?*

   - *How did you feel toward your body?*

- *What were your thoughts about the body?*

- *What part of this exercise was helpful?*

- *Was there anything that was difficult? Did anything make your laugh?*

- *When did you feel joy?*

8. Help your client reflect on the experiences of joy, however brief, during this exercise. Ask:

    Were you able, just for a moment, to let go of thoughts of self-harm?

9. Summarize what you have done today:

    - Your client has learned to be mindfully and joyfully present in the body.

    - She has learned to "let go" for a moment and just be.

    - She let herself experience brief moments of joy being present with her body and in the presence of another human being.

10. Assign homework: Ask your client to build moments of joyful presence into each day. Joyful motion is a great way to let go of the day when it ends. Joy doesn't get rid of thoughts of self-harm, but it can be a powerful antidote and can counterbalance those thoughts. Say to your client:

    You deserve to experience joy, and you can create joy in this simple way.

Give your client the following chart to keep her on track with completing homework. For right now, ask her to create one joyful dance moment per day. Remember: This does not require a lot of time. Perhaps two minutes will do.

If your client has younger children, it may be fun to ask them to join in.

Joyful Presence through Motion:		
Monday:		
Tuesday:		
Wednesday:		
Thursday:		
Friday:		
Saturday:		
Sunday:		

Figure 33

11. Closing: Remind your client that learning joyful presence takes time. You
    can say:

    - *It's OK if this feels silly.*

    - *Just give it a try.*

    - *Over time, this will be more and more fun.*

Psychoeducation Interventions

Knowledge really can be power. When trauma has taken over a life, it can also take away, at least partially, the ability to think clearly, to think things through, to remember what was formerly known. Your client may not be able to recall information because her entire life was shaped by experiences of trauma and toxic stress. She may have missed out on information that was easily accessible to others. The following interventions focus on three areas in which psychoeducation may be needed:

- psychoeducation about the impact of trauma on the body and brain;
- healthy relationships; and
- living a healthy life.

You should assess which information is most important for your client and begin there. For example: If your client struggles with falling and staying asleep, start there. If your client cannot sleep, it is unlikely that she will be able to think clearly, make good decisions, and learn new material.

INTERVENTION 8

Minding the Body

This intervention is designed to help your client explore and understand the impact trauma has had in his body and brain. Together, you will assess how your client feels and thinks, and you will help him understand in what ways his thoughts and feelings relate to his traumatic experience.

Target skill: Insight. Decision making. Problem solving.

What you will need: Outline of the body. Writing tools, colored pencils, crayons. Here is a body outline you can use:

Figure 34

1.   Begin with empathy. Ask your client the following kinds of questions:

   - *Are there parts of your body that hurt and you don't know why?*

   - *Do you get sick often?*

   - *Are you more tired than most people?*

   - *Do you sometimes feel like you don't belong in your own skin?*

   Listen reflectively. Find out how your client relates to his body. Ask:

   - *Does your body feel like a stranger to you?*

   - *Does your body feel like a burden?*

- *Does it feel like your body is fighting you?*
- *Do you feel like you are fighting your body?*
- *How much agitation do you feel in your body?*
- *Are you ever kind to your body?*
- *Do you listen to the messages your body gives you? If you do, how do you relate to those messages?*

When you are asking these kinds of questions, you are communicating that there are different ways of relating to the body.

2. **Introduce today's task:** understanding the impact of trauma on the body and the brain.

3. Provide psychoeducation. Use the following script:

   The body and the brain are connected in intricate ways. People who have been hurt, who have experienced trauma, often find that their relationship with their body has changed. This is because trauma really can change the messages the brain and the body exchange.

   Trauma can put your biology on high alert.

   Your body produces stress hormones that can keep you on high alert even when the danger is over.

   When your body has been on high alert for a long time, you can get very tired. The body is not designed to manage constant feelings of danger.

   Your body may "flip" between being on high alert and being very, very tired.

   This is a biological response to stress. You are not doing this.

   You can reset this response over time.

   All of this can make you feel estranged from your body. Like your body is doing all these things and you can't control them. But it is possible to be kind to the body and feel at home in it again over time. This is what our work is about. You can change the way your body responds over time—not by fighting it, but by giving it what it needs. It's like resetting the clock.

4. Work on today's task: Give your client the body outline. Of course, he can make his own, if he wants to.

Figure 35

Ask your client to describe what is going on in his body. Which parts are most comfortable? What hurts? What does he do to feel better when part of his body hurts? Use the outline to create a map of how your client relates to his body and what it may need. Use colors to mark pain. It's OK to be metaphorical. Here are a few examples of what you could say:

- *Perhaps it feels like there is an elephant sitting on your shoulders.*

- *Perhaps it feels like you are always in motion, running away from a lion.*

- *Perhaps it feels like bees are buzzing around your body/brain all the time.*

5. Once you have identified where and how your client's traumatic experiences live in the body, you can help him develop ways of responding. Explain by saying things like:

- *It's best to be kind to the body.*

- *There are some basic things your body needs, like food and sleep.*

- *Let's make a plan to give the body what it needs.*

You can use the following chart:

What my body needs:	What I can do about this:	When can I do this:

Figure 36

Here are some examples:

What my body needs:	What I can do about this:	When can I do this:
Perhaps the body needs more sleep.	I can set a bedtime.	Every night.
	I can learn to relax my body.	
	I can be kind to my body.	

Figure 37

Be sure to help your client be specific. If your client is working on learning to relax his body, explain that this will take time. Identify three things your client can learn to do, such as belly breathing, listening to music, and taking a warm bath.

You can say something like:

You are changing your relationship to your body. Trauma has changed it in ways that are unwanted, and you are changing it back. This will take time. In the meantime, be kind to yourself.

6. Summarize what you have done so far: You have explored together the impact that trauma has had on your client's body and the way he relates to it. You have identified ways in which your client can begin to be kind to his body and help it regulate responses. You have created a list of things your

client can do. Most importantly, you have explored the need to be kind to the body.

7. Assign homework: Ask your client to pick one thing from the list you created together. It could be the thing that is most important to him, bothers him the most, or is easiest to change. Mark your client's choice with a highlighter and ask him to engage, every day, in ways to be kind to the body to address the issue. If your client needs more ideas, help him develop them now. Send the list home with him. You may want to laminate it. Ask your client to bring the list back to your next meeting.

8. Closing: Be sure to send your client home with words of encouragement. You can say things like:

    - *You can be at home in your body.*

    - *Your body can be your friend.*

    - *Be kind to yourself and your body.*

INTERVENTION 9

Minding Feelings: Soothing

When there is trauma, inevitably, there is the need to soothe. Maladaptive ways of soothing are widely available: Food, electronic distractions, sex and pornography, legal and illegal drugs, alcohol. Many of these are potentially addicting. When your client struggles with a trauma-related disorder and an addiction, you will need to treat both concurrently. Helping your client learn to self-soothe is a component of treatment for both PTSD and addiction. Of course, you need to make sure that all the other components needed are in place.

There is often a great deal of shame around addiction. Yet, from a trauma perspective, addiction is logical. If there was something to ease your emotional and physical pain, why wouldn't you use it, especially if it seems to "work" right away? The message to your clients should be: "I understand. Pain can drive people into addiction. Addiction then takes over. It has its own dynamic. I understand you were not looking for an addiction. You were looking for a way to feel better."

Learning to self-soothe can be cumbersome. Substances work so much quicker. Be sure to help your client understand that learning to self-soothe takes time.

Target skill: Soothing. Insight.

What you will need: Ability to co-regulate intense affective states. Bag of tricks: This is a bag full of items that can be used for self-soothing: stress ball, blanket, stuffed animals, beautiful images, music. The goal is to build a bag over time that is specific to your client.

1. Begin with empathy. Ask your client questions like:

   - *Do you ever feel out of control?*

   - *Can it be difficult to make yourself feel better?*

   - *Are your emotions very intense?*

   Listen reflectively. Then reframe difficulties in affect regulation as symptoms of trauma exposure. Say: "It makes sense that you struggle with intense emotions. This is a symptom. It's not your fault."

2. **Introduce today's task:** learning to feel better using self-soothing.

3. Review last week's homework. Ask questions like:

   - *In what ways were you kind to your body?*

   - *How did you feel when you were kind to your body?*

   - *What worked? What did not work?*

   - *If there were barriers to being kind to your body, what were they? How can you overcome them?*

4. Work on today's task: learning about and beginning to practice self-soothing.

5. Provide psychoeducation about the connection between trauma and intense emotions. Here is what you can say:

The body and the brain are connected in intricate ways. People who have been hurt, who have experienced trauma, often find it difficult to recognize and manage their feelings. This is because trauma is so overwhelming that trauma survivors move into a survival state. In a survival state, you can't pay too much attention to how you feel.

Trauma can put your biology on high alert.

Your body produces stress hormones that can keep you on high alert even when the danger is over.

When you are on high alert, feelings get pushed to the side.

If this happens when you are a child, it can become difficult to know what feelings are, let alone understand and manage them.

This can lead to feeling overwhelmed and confused.

All of this can make you feel estranged from yourself and your feelings. But it is possible to learn to recognize and soothe intense feelings. This is what the work is about. You can change the way you respond over time. You don't have to fight your feelings. You can recognize them and manage them.

6. Begin by helping your client understand the process. Here is an image to help:

Figure 38

The key here is to respond to feelings mindfully, to take a break before acting on them—in essence, to separate feelings from impulsive responses to them.

7. Introduce the idea of building a self-soothing bag. Take out the bag that you have and ask your client to examine its contents. Ask which one of the items could be helpful when there is a need to self-soothe.

8. Make it concrete. Ask your client to think of a distressing situation, but not the most distressing situation. You are practicing. You want your client to succeed.

9. Ask your client to describe her emotional response to the situation, then rate the intensity of her feelings using the following rating arrow.

Figure 39

10. Ask your client to pick up her favorite item from the bag and use it for self-soothing. You may have to help your client narrate what she is doing. Here are some examples of things she can say to herself:

   - *I am using this blanket to wrap myself. I am feeling out of control and will comfort myself in this way.*

   - *I am so very mad right now. I am using this stress ball to let go, slowly, of my rage.*

   Help your client notice that you are breaking the instant connection between feelings and actions.

11. Use the feelings rating arrow again. If your client's feelings-intensity level came down just one point, this is success. If it did not, choose a different item from the bag, or explore what is missing from the bag and needs to go in it.

12. Summarize what you have done today: Your client has learned about the connection between intense emotions and trauma. You have begun to explore how to soothe emotions using comfort items.

13. Assign homework: Ask your client to pick her favorite item for soothing from the bag and take it home. Also send home a copy of the feelings rating arrow. Ask your client to use the comfort item when she has overwhelming feelings, then use the feelings arrow to check off and record intensity of feelings before and after using the comfort item. She should bring the item and the feelings arrow back to your next meeting.

14. Ultimately, you want your client to build her own bag of tricks for self-soothing.

15. Closing: Send your client home with words of encouragement. You can say things like:

   - *Feelings can be recognized.*

   - *Feelings can be accepted.*

   - *Feelings can be contained.*

   - *You can soothe your intense feelings.*

   - *Practice makes perfect!*

INTERVENTION 10

Minding the Brain

This intervention is designed to help your client explore and understand how trauma can impact the brain. Your client may not understand that he is forgetful or can't think well because trauma has put his brain and body into a fight/flight or freeze response. When this happens, remembering and thinking take a back seat out of necessity. Your client's entire being is in a biologically driven state enabling survival. When survival is at stake, there is no time to think.

1. Begin with empathy. Ask questions like:

   - *How was your week?*

   - *In what ways were you able to be kind to yourself?*

   - *How did you feel when you were kind to your body?*

   - *In what way was your body your friend this week?*

2. **Introduce today's task:** understanding the fight/flight/freeze respond to threat.

3. Review last week's homework: Take a look at the chart together, specifically the highlighted area. Ask questions like:

   - In what way were you able to attend to your body in a helpful way?

   - How did this change your relationship with your body?

   - What feelings came up? Joy? Shame? Guilt? Fear? Contentment?

   Normalize feelings that came up. If your client felt ashamed or undeserving about taking care of his body, reframe the shame as an old message from trauma. Explain that the messages trauma sends are not always true. Ask your client to continue to work his way through his chart. Reinforce his need to be kind to the body and to himself.

4. Work on today's task: Provide psychoeducation. Say this:

   When there is danger, the body is designed to shut down all areas that are not essential for survival. When there is danger, we are designed to run, fight, freeze, or hide. Here are the things that we don't do well when there is danger: We may struggle to solve problems, think things through, make complex decisions, or remember important things.

   Just think about it: If a lion was attacking you and you took time to think things through, you would not survive. Our bodies are designed to respond to danger as if every danger was a lion. Our brains may "shut off" during times of extreme stress. If we have extreme stress for a long time, problem solving, thinking things through, making complex decisions, and remembering things can become more difficult. This is not your fault. This is a biological response.

   All of this can make you feel estranged from your brain, like your brain is doing all of these things and you can't control it. But it is possible to be kind to the brain and feel at home in it. This is what the work is about. You can change the way your brain responds over time—not by fighting it, but by giving it what it needs. It's like resetting the clock.

5. You can use the body outline to further explain how the brain/body responds to stress. This may be especially helpful with children. You can add to this image:

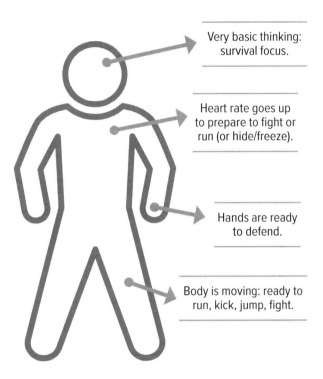

Very basic thinking: survival focus.

Heart rate goes up to prepare to fight or run (or hide/freeze).

Hands are ready to defend.

Body is moving: ready to run, kick, jump, fight.

Figure 40

Help your client add to this image. Ask: "What happens to you?"

6. Once you understand where your client's traumatic experiences "sit" in the brain, you can help him develop ways of responding. Explain:

It's best to be kind to the brain. There are some basic things your brain needs. Curiously, they can be similar to what the body needs, things like food and sleep. But then there are other things: The brain needs time to rest. The brain needs interesting things to think about. The brain needs interaction with others. Let's make a plan to give the brain what it needs.

You can use the following chart:

What my brain needs:	What I can do about this:	When can I do this:

Figure 41

Here are some examples:

What my brain needs:	What I can do about this:	When can I do this:
The brain needs interaction with others	I can meet with . . .	Once every day
	I can call . . .	
	I can be kind to my brain . . .	

Figure 42

Be sure to help your client be specific. If your client is working on learning to relax his brain, explain that this will take time. Identify three things your client can learn to do, such as listening to calm music, reading a good book, and using positive affirmations.

You can say something like:

> *You are changing your relationship to your brain. Trauma has changed it in ways that are unwanted, and you are changing it back. This will take time. In the meantime, be kind to yourself.*

7.   Summarize what you have done so far:

   • You have explored together the impact that trauma has had on your client's brain and the way he relates to it.

- You have identified ways in which your client can begin to be kind to his brain and give his brain what it needs.

- You have created a list of things your client can do.

- Most importantly, you have explored the need to be kind to the brain.

8. Assign homework: Ask your client to pick one thing from the list you created together. It could be the thing that is most important to him, bothers him the most, or is easiest to change. Mark your client's choice with a highlighter and ask him to engage, every day, in ways to be kind to the brain to address the issue. If your client needs more ideas, help him develop them now. Send the list home with him. You may want to laminate it. Ask your client to bring the chart back to your next meeting.

9. Closing: Be sure to send your client home with words of encouragement. You can say things like:

    - Your brain can be your friend.

    - It's all in there. You just have to give your brain what it needs for a while.

    - Be kind to yourself and your body and your brain.

INTERVENTION 11

Being with Yourself

Trauma, especially developmental trauma, alters the way a person relates to other people. Your client may have a difficult time trusting others. Your client may, in fact, not know how to relate to others or understand that attachment builds healthy humans and healthy relationships.

If your client's experience has been that no one is truly there for her, then she may look at the people around her not as a source of nurturance and healing, but as an assortment of people. Additionally, if your client has not learned to truly love and be loved, her relationship with herself can be difficult. It may be devoid of compassion and the ability to relate to herself as a lovable human being.

This intervention addresses the lack of connection to oneself that trauma can create. Of course, this intervention is only a start. Building a compassionate relationship with oneself takes time.

Target skill: Self compassion. Acceptance.

What you will need: Paper, colored pencils, crayons, glue, craft materials, photos of client (if available and appropriate).

1. Begin with empathy. Ask questions like:

    - *How was your week?*

    - *In what ways were you able to be kind to yourself?*

    - *How did you feel when you were kind to your brain?*

    - *In what way was your brain your friend this week?*

2. **Introduce today's task:** learning self-compassion.

3. Review last week's homework: Take a look at the chart together, specifically the highlighted area. Ask the following kinds of questions:

    - In what way where you able to attend to your brain in a helpful way?

    - How did this change your relationship with your brain?

    - What feelings came up? Joy? Shame? Guilt? Fear? Contentment? Curiosity?

    Normalize feelings that came up. If your client felt ashamed or undeserving about taking care of her brain, reframe the shame as an old message from trauma. Explain that the messages trauma sends are not always true. Ask your client to continue to work her way through her chart.

    - Reinforce the need to be kind to the body, to the brain, and to herself.

4. Ask if your client needs any more information about trauma and the brain. If she does, you may want to provide a diagram with simple information about trauma and the brain/body. You can use Child Welfare's *Understanding the Effects of Maltreatment on Brain Development* as a basis for your discussion. Visit www.childwelfare.gov/pubPDFs/brain_development.pdf for handouts.

5. Introduce today's task: being with oneself with kindness, acceptance, and compassion.

6. Provide psychoeducation. Say some things like this:

    Trauma can change the way you feel and think about yourself. Trauma may tell you that you are unlovable and unworthy. If most of your life has been traumatic, trauma may have told you that you are all alone; there is no one to help you or to love you, and that there is no possibility of love in the world.

    You may have learned that you can never show kindness or weakness. When trauma is all around, this makes sense. When people are in survival mode, they cannot think about how they feel. They just act to protect themselves the best they can.

    Yet, it is possible to pay attention to yourself with kindness and compassion. As you are and feel safer and safer, you can attend to who you are, what you feel, and how you relate to yourself. It will probably feel strange to be kind to yourself in the beginning. That's OK. Being kind and compassionate to yourself will take time and practice.

7. Work on today's task: You can use the following image to help your client. Your client can also draw herself or use a photo of herself. Let your client be as creative about this as possible. Taking time to develop a drawing/image of oneself already is one way to be kind to oneself.

Kind thoughts about Myself:

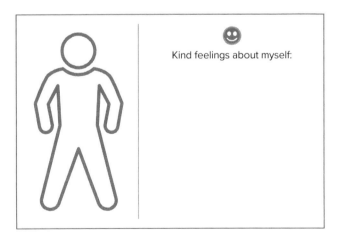

Kind feelings about myself:

Figure 43

8. If and when trauma-based thoughts and feelings intrude into the image, take out another piece of paper and label it: "Trauma-based thoughts and feelings about myself." Ask your client to write those thoughts and feelings on this different piece of paper. In this way your client can begin to reflect on

the fact that trauma-based thoughts and feelings are just messages trauma has given. They may have been self-protective, but they are no longer needed or appropriate to the situation.

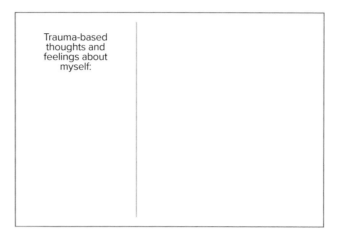

Figure 44

While your client creates the image of herself, be curious and ask reflective questions. Help your client understand that she can develop a kind and compassionate relationship with herself over time.

9. When your client has completed the image, help her explore the idea of a relationship with herself. You can explain that being kind, compassionate, and accepting is part of the process of building a new relationship with herself. This relationship will include:

    •   compassion, kindness, and acceptance.

    •   getting to know new thoughts, feelings, and behaviors that are not trauma-based.

    •   examining trauma-based thoughts, feelings, and behaviors, and gaining distance from them without judgment.

10. Summarize what you have done so far: You have explored what a kind, compassionate, and accepting relationship with oneself may look like.

11. Ask your client to name one thing she can do over the next week to develop a kind, compassionate, and accepting relationship with herself.

12. Assign homework: Ask your client to engage in the specific thing she has chosen to do in order to be kind, compassionate, and accepting toward herself once every day.

13. If your client is struggling with identifying ideas, that's OK. Here are a few examples:

    •   positive affirmations such as: *I deserve to love and to be loved.*

- making time to create happiness when alone: listening to music, making a collage.

- making time to think about new ways of being.

14. Give your client the following chart to keep track of her efforts. Ask her to bring it to your next meeting.

I will be kind to myself by . . .
Monday:
Tuesday:
Wednesday:
Thursday:
Friday:
Saturday:
Sunday:

Figure 45

15. Closing: Send your client home with words of encouragement. You can say things like:

- *You can be kind, compassionate, and accepting toward yourself.*

- *You deserve to take time to develop a new relationship with yourself.*

INTERVENTION 12

Being with Others

Trauma, especially developmental trauma, alters the way a person relates to other people. Your client may have a difficult time trusting others. Your client may, in fact, not know how to relate to others or understand the importance of attachment. If your client's experience has been that no one is truly there for him, then he may not see the people around him as a source of nurturance and healing. This intervention addresses the lack of connection to others that trauma can create. Of course, this intervention is only a start. Building compassionate relationships takes time.

Target skill: Being with others. Connection.

What you will need: Paper. Drawing and writing tools. Craft materials. Index cards.

1. Begin with empathy. Ask questions like:

   - *How was your week?*

   - *In what ways were you able to be kind to yourself?*

   - *How did you feel when you were kind to yourself?*

   - *In what way were you your own friend this week?*

2. **Introduce today's task:** learning to be with others and making plans for this.

3. Review last week's homework: Take a look at the chart together, specifically the highlighted area. Ask questions like:

   - *In what way where you to be kind and compassionate toward yourself?*

   - *How did this change your relationship with yourself?*

   - *What feelings came up? Joy? Shame? Guilt? Fear? Contentment? Curiosity?*

   - *Normalize feelings that came up. If your client felt ashamed or undeserving about attending to his relationship with himself, reframe the shame as an old message from trauma. Explain that the messages trauma sends are not always true.*

   - *Reinforce the need to be kind to the body and the brain.*

4. Work on today's task: Provide psychoeducation. Trauma can change the way you feel and think about yourself. Educate your client by saying things like:

   - *Trauma may tell you that you are unlovable and unworthy. If most of your life has been traumatic, trauma may have told you that you are all alone; there is no one to help you or to love you, and that there is no possibility of love in the world.*

   - *You may have learned that you can never show kindness or weakness. When trauma is all around, this makes sense. When people are in survival mode, they cannot think about how they feel. They just act to protect themselves the best they can. It's difficult to develop kind, compassionate, and accepting relationships when you are in survival mode.*

- *However, it is possible to pay attention to others with kindness and compassion. As you are and feel safer, you can now attend to who you are, what you feel, and how you relate to others.*

- *It will probably feel strange to relate to others with compassion, kindness, and acceptance in the beginning. That's OK. Being kind and compassionate will take time and practice. This is a new way of being for you that is not trauma-based. It will take time to learn.*

5. Ask your client to reflect on kind, compassionate, and accepting relationships. What do they look like? Has she ever seen any? What characteristics do they have? You can use the following image, a kind of relationship compass, to help your client reflect:

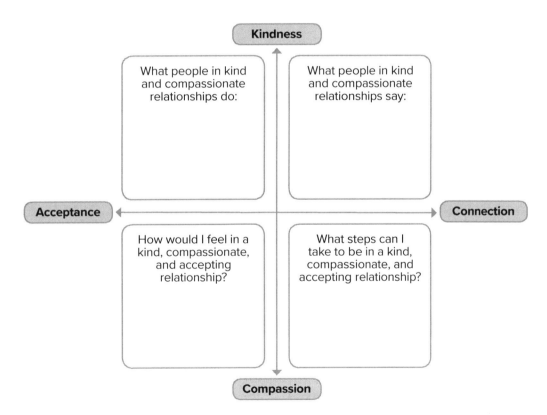

Figure 46

Your client can write on the compass. If there is not enough space, you can add index cards on each side. Your client can also draw or add pictures. If trauma-based ideas about relationships with others come up, simply write them on a separate index card:

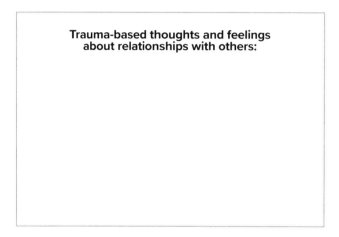

Figure 47

In this way your client can begin to reflect on the fact that trauma-based thoughts and feelings are just that: They are based on messages trauma has given. They may have been self-protective, but they are no longer needed or appropriate to the situation.

6. Summarize what you have done: You have learned about the impact of trauma on relationships with others. You have reflected on what compassionate, kind, and accepting relationships with others look like.

7. Assign homework: Give your client the following worksheet to complete and bring back to your next meeting:

	Person:	**Person:**
What in this relationship is kind, compassionate and accepting:		
What in this relationship is trauma-based?		

Figure 48

Remind your client to be compassionate with himself when reflecting about this. This homework is not about shaming oneself over relationship mistakes. Rather, it is about building (what is kind, compassionate, and accepting) and pruning (what is hurtful and trauma-based).

8. Closing: Send your client home with words of encouragement. You can say things like:

    • *You can be fine and build kind, compassionate, and accepting relationships.*

    • *You deserve to be in kind, compassionate, and accepting relationships.*

INTERVENTION 13

Being Well

What does it mean to be healthy? Someone who has experienced trauma, especially developmental trauma, may not know that humans need adequate sleep. If you don't sleep enough, you can't be well.

We need food. The right kind. Stress drives you to eat foods that don't nurture the body well.

We need connection. Trauma can separate you from yourself and others.

This intervention helps your client understand her basic human needs so that she can begin to recognize them in her daily life. Of course, this intervention does not constitute medical advice. If necessary, be sure to refer her to a medical provider.

Target skill: Knowledge about needs. Making space for needs.

What you will need: Paper. Writing tools. Highlighter.

1. Begin with empathy. Ask questions like:

   - *How was your week?*

   - *In what way did you connect with others?*

   - *How did you feel when you connected with others?*

   - *In what way were you your own friend this week?*

2. **Introduce today's task:** learning to be well.

3. Review last week's homework. Look at your client's relationship worksheet together. Review:

   - What were the kind, compassionate, and accepting elements in her relationships?

   - Recognize the trauma-based elements in relationships.

   - Help your client accept that building kind, compassionate, and accepting relationships can take time.

   - Ask your client to connect more with people who provide elements of kindness, compassion, and acceptance.

4. Work on today's task: Provide psychoeducation. Here is what you can say:

   Trauma puts you into survival mode. When you are in survival mode, being well is not important. Survival is important. In survival mode you might not:

   - *eat well. When you are in survival mode, you eat high-calorie, high-sugar foods for quick energy. This makes sense when you have to outrun a tiger. Biology tells you to eat high-calorie, high-sugar foods when you are under stress. Your stress is different. You need to eat to be well.*

   - *sleep well or enough. When you are in survival mode you must be aware of what is going on around you at all times. You are always looking for danger, including at night. In order to recover from trauma, you will need to learn to sleep enough and sleep well. This will take time. Be patient with yourself.*

- be connected. *When you are in survival mode, you expect danger from anyone at any time. This makes it difficult to have close and trusting relationships. In order to recover from trauma, you will need to learn to connect with safe friends. Learning to recognize safe friends and building trust will take time. Be patient with yourself.*

5. Help your client create a "Be Well Chart." Please note that this chart is just the beginning. It is a visual tool to help your client understand what it means to be well. You will need to work with your client on integrating steps to being well into her life over the course of her treatment.

You can use the following chart:

Be Well Chart		
To eat well, I will:	To sleep well, I will:	To be connected, I will:

Figure 49

Help your client make things concrete. Ask:

- *When are you going to do this?*
- *How are you going to do this?*

If needed, provide more psychoeducation. Here is an example: It is quite common for people who are anxious to distract themselves using electronic devices. They essentially use the device until they are so exhausted that they "pass out" instead of fall asleep. You may have to tell your client that while electronic devices provide distraction, they are not helpful when it comes to establishing good sleep hygiene. When the mind doesn't have a chance to let go, it is busy until there is sleep. Under these circumstances sleep is likely to be less restful.

6. Summarize what you have done so far:

    - Your client has learned about the impact trauma can have on the ability to meet one's own needs.

    - Your client has explored what it means to take good care of her eating and sleeping habits as well as her way of connecting with others.

7. Explore: How does it feel to pay attention to the basics of eating, sleeping, and connecting?

8. Assign homework: Ask your client to take a look at the chart you just created and pick one element she is willing and able to tackle. Highlight that element. Ask your client to complete a specific task related to that element on a daily basis over the next week and then check off completion on the following chart. Ask your client to bring the chart back to your next meeting.

I will practice being well by . . .
Monday:
Tuesday:
Wednesday:
Thursday:
Friday:
Saturday:
Sunday:

Figure 50

9. Close the meeting with kind words like:

    - *You can learn to be well step by step.*

    - *If it feels strange at first, that's OK.*

    - *You will feel better when you take good care of yourself.*

Skill Building Interventions

Skill building is an essential component in the treatment of trauma symptoms. When people experience trauma, they move into an altered state of body and mind, essentially into a survival state. Using an elaborate set of interpersonal and other skills is not essential in a life-threatening situation. When the only thing that is important is survival, the fight/flight or freeze response kicks in. Once this response is in place, it can be difficult to turn off. Even if your client understands that the danger is over, his body may remain in a survival state.

If your client's entire development was characterized by the presence of trauma and toxic stress—as may be the case when children are repeatedly abused and neglected—he may never have had a chance to build age-appropriate interpersonal and life skills. You can think of this as a developmental delay. Your 21-year-old client may have the interpersonal and life skills of a 10-year-old. People who have experienced trauma commonly lack:

- life skills such as organizational skills;
- interpersonal skills; and
- affect regulation skills.

There are some other things your client may be able to do exceptionally well. Your client may be very adept at "reading" people. This is often an intuitive skill developed to stay safe and survive. If you live in a violent home, reading people can be very useful as you would better know when to hide. But the skill of reading people is often very selective. Your client may be able to sense danger but unable to scan for kindness, compassion, and love. Skills that are necessary for survival and safety may be overdeveloped, while others are weak.

INTERVENTION 14

Life Skills 101: Having a Plan

When you are in survival mode, planning is not first on your list. You simply run or hide. But our clients need planning skills to survive in the real world. In the real world we live according to schedules. You often have to be on time, register for classes, pay your bills. It is important that your client gain or maintain as much stability as possible while she recovers from her traumatic experiences. If life is unstable, chances are your client will experience more stress.

Begin by helping your client have a plan. This plan can take many forms. It can address a specific time frame or need. Make adjustments to fit your client. It may take several sessions and several plans to help your client build the specific planning skills she needs.

Target skill: Foresight. Planning. Attention to values and needs.

What you will need: Poster board or paper. Index cards. Writing tools such as markers, crayons. Children and creative adults can decorate their plans; in this case you would need additional art/craft materials.

1. Begin with empathy. Ask your client:

   - *How easy is it for you to plan ahead?*

   - *How prepared are you to take on the things you need to take on every day?*

   - *What kinds of experiences have you had that led you to question your ability to manage things?*

   - *How do you feel about your ability to manage your life?*

   Listen reflectively. Explain: "Trauma can rob you of your ability to make a plan. This is a symptom, not a personal fault."

2. **Introduce today's task:** learning to make and use a plan.

3. Review last week's homework. Ask your client to take out her Be Well chart and take a look together.

   - How many times was your client able to engage in an activity designed to help her be well?

   - How did she feel when she engaged in the activity?

   - When she was not able to engage in the activity, what got in the way? What was the barrier?

   - Explore how barriers can be removed.

   - Set a realistic goal. Perhaps engaging in the activity five out of seven days will work for your client. Keep in mind that you want self-care to become a habit. This may not work if your client only engages in the activity every once in a while.

4. Work on today's task: Provide psychoeducation. Here is what you can say:

Trauma puts you into survival mode. When you are in survival mode, making a plan is not important. You may not:

- plan ahead to for paying your bills, being on time and the like.

- know how to make and follow a plan at all. Trauma tells you to scan for danger at all times. But in order to recover from your traumatic experience, you will need to learn to plan. Trauma brings chaos. Chaos creates more chaos. Planning reduces chaos and insecurity.

- understand the importance of planning. It may seem like a waste of time, especially if you are expecting that things will go wrong no matter what you do. Planning decreases the need for further planning. Planning is your friend!

Use the example of getting a job. You should pick a task that is specific to your client and repeat this activity several times until she has demonstrated that she is able to make a plan by herself.

5. You can use the following chart to help your client make a plan:

Overall Goal: Obtain Meaningful Employment			
Step 1: Clarification of goal	What kind of employment?	What skills do I have? What skills do I need to gain?	How can I gain those skills?
Date to begin:			
Date to finish:			
Step 2: Action Plan	Gaining skills: Register for classes, when and where?	Complete training.	Identify jobs to apply for that I am now qualified for:
Date to begin:			
Date to finish:			
Step 3: Moving ahead	Complete job applications (at least 5) and follow up after a week.	Interview and or send out more applications.	Accept and prepare for position.
Date to begin:			
Date to finish			

Figure 51

As you are creating this plan with your client, be sure to assign dates to all tasks for completion.

6. If your client struggles with planning, be reassuring. Remind your client:

   - This is a skill that can be learned.

   - You may not have this skill yet because of your traumatic life experiences.

   - This is not your fault.

   - Practice makes perfect.

7. As you are making a plan, help your client understand and reflect on the following things:

   - how planning relates to her values.

   - how planning relates to her sense of self-efficacy (her feelings that she can tackle and accomplish something).

   - how planning relates to the way she values her own life and assigns importance to it.

   In other words: Planning is not important for the sake of planning. Planning embodies what is important to your client, what she feels needs to get done and the importance she assigns to herself.

8. Review what you have done so far: You have explored how trauma has impacted your client's ability to plan ahead. You have identified a goal for your client and made this goal come to life by creating a visual plan that includes an outline and a timeline. You have explored why planning is important and how it relates to your client's sense of self.

9. Assign homework: Go back to the planning chart. Ask your client to "work" the chart by picking the first few tasks to accomplish over the next week. Your client may only be able to accomplish one task. This is OK. You want her to be successful. Highlight the assigned task, and write it and its completion date on an index card and send it home with your client. She should post the index card as a reminder in a prominent place. Give your client additional index cards to take notes about completing the task. Ask her to bring all index cards to your next meeting.

10. Closing: Leave your client with words of encouragement, like:

    - *Planning helps you value yourself.*

    - *Planning can help you banish chaos in your life.*

    - *Planning is a skill you can learn. It might take time.*

    - *Planning can help you find your place in the world.*

INTERVENTION 15

Life Skills 101: Having a Life Plan

This intervention more broadly addresses the need to have a plan for one's life. Planning can be difficult for trauma survivors, but it can be eye-opening. When you are making such a plan you are asking:

- What is my life really about?

- What do I do well?

- Which direction am I going?

- What do I want to build?

- What do I value?

All of these questions ask your client to step away from chaos toward reflection. Making a plan means that you don't accept *what is* as the only option for the future, and that you recognize that you can build the life that you want (to the extent that any of us can).

Target skill: Reflection. Planning. Identifying values and purpose.

What you will need: Poster board or paper. Writing tools such as markers, crayons. If you are working with a child (or a creative adult) your client can decorate his plan in order to relate to it better, to make it his own. In this case you would need additional art/craft materials. Index cards.

1. Begin with empathy. Ask questions like:

   - *How was the last week?*

   - *What went well?*

   - *What did you do that made things go well?*

   - *In what way did you create meaning in your life?*

   - *When things did not go well, what did you think? What did you do?*

   Use reflective listening to mirror your client's ability to take active and positive steps in his life.

2. **Introduce today's task:** creating a life plan. You can explain that plans can be changed as needed, but having an overall plan is helpful.

3. Review last week's homework. Ask your client to take a look at his homework index card with you. Did he accomplish his task? If he did, what is the next task? When will this be completed? Set a pace that works for your client, and take external pressures into account. If your client has no source of income, finding employment will need to be practical and fast.

   If your client was not able to accomplish the task, what stood in the way? What needs to happen for the barrier to be removed? Was the task too ambitious? Was it not a priority? Was it the wrong task?

4. Work on today's task: Provide psychoeducation. Say something like:

Trauma puts you into survival mode. When you are in survival mode, making a plan is not important. You might not:

- *plan ahead to pay your bills, be on time and the like.*

- *think and reflect about your life enough to create a plan.*

- *know how to make and follow a plan at all. Trauma tells you to scan for danger at all times. Trauma considers planning a distraction to this. But to recover you will need to learn to plan. Trauma brings chaos. Chaos creates more chaos. Planning reduces chaos and insecurity.*

- *understand the importance of planning. It may seem like a waste of time, especially if you are expecting that things will go wrong no matter what you do. Planning decreases the need for further planning. Planning is your friend!*

5. Begin by identifying values. If the term *values* is too abstract for your client, ask: Who and what are most important to you? You can use the following image to help with this:

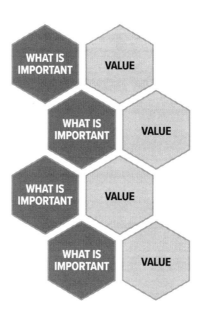

Figure 52

6. You can think of these elements as pieces of a puzzle. From the puzzle pieces you and your client will be able to extract values. Let's say the puzzle pieces are:

- Mom. My children. My partner. Yoga group. Movies and books.

Your values may be:

- Connection. Family. Education. Nurturing self.

7. Once you have identified two to three basic values, help your client begin his life plan. You should explain that plans are meant to be flexible. Circumstances change, and plans based on identified values may change.

This image can help with beginning a life plan:

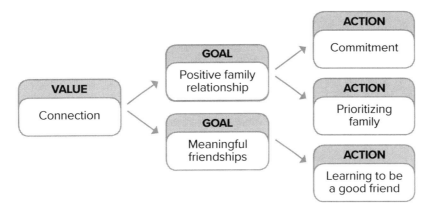

Figure 53

You can see how you will be able to branch out into more concrete steps. Identifying values can also help your client recognize when he is off course. If, for example, your client often complains about his friends, you can ask: In what way are you creating meaningful friendships? How are your friends contributing to meaningful friendships?

8. In the end, you want to end up with a plan that spells out values, goals, and actions. Here is an empty form to use with your client:

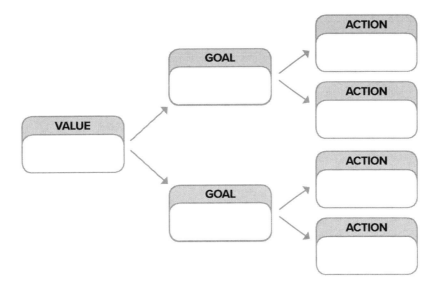

Figure 54

9. Once again: Help your client reflect on the ways in which he is now taking action in his life, instead of letting trauma plant chaos. Additionally, ask questions like:

- *In what way are you assigning importance to yourself and your role in this world by making a life plan?*

- *What do you think your mission in life may be?*

- *In what way can you be flexible with this plan?*

10. Summarize what you have done so far. You have explored the ways in which trauma has kept your client from planning ahead. You have explored the benefits of creating a life plan and have used your client's values to begin to build one. You have also explored the importance of flexibility when creating a plan.

11. Assign homework: Ask your client to pick one of his values. Give him an index card and ask him to record the actions he takes every day to bring that value to life.

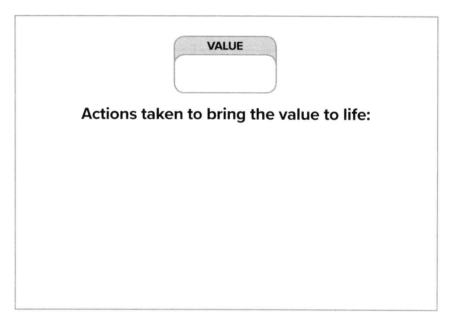

Figure 55

12. Closing: Send your client home with words of encouragement, like:

- *Taking thoughtful action will make a difference.*

- *You can walk into the direction of the life you want.*

- *Setting goals and following through just takes practice. No need to be perfect right away.*

Interpersonal Skills Interventions

These are skills that help you create and maintain meaningful connections. People who have experienced trauma may be suspicious of interpersonal connections. They may struggle to read people, to listen and respond appropriately, and to make themselves clear.

Your client's experience may be that people just hurt people. Hence connections are dangerous as opposed to nurturing and meaningful.

To make connections you must have skills. You must be able to read people accurately, to respond to them in the right way. You must know when to walk away and how to listen. You must know how to make yourself heard. If you have experienced trauma, especially as a child, you may only know some of those skills, or you may not know them at all.

A comprehensive list of interpersonal skills and interventions related to them is beyond the scope of this manual. We will focus on three domains that trauma survivors frequently struggle with:

- boundaries;

- being heard and having a voice; and

- managing feelings in relationships.

INTERVENTION 16

My Space

This intervention addresses the need to establish healthy boundaries in relationships. This can be difficult for trauma survivors. They may have learned that they are not allowed to establish their own boundaries and that it may, in fact, be dangerous to try. Alternatively, they may have learned to be in their own space so much that they have lost touch with others. This is protective: If others can't come close, they can't be a source of pain. This intervention is about the happy medium, healthy boundaries that allow for connection and space.

Target skill: Creating and maintaining healthy boundaries. Assertiveness.

What you will need: Space (enough to stretch out arms without bumping into walls). Paper and writing/drawing tools. Index cards.

1. Begin with empathy. Ask questions like:

   - *How was the last week?*

   - *How are you doing in your relationships?*

   - *What is comfortable in relationships?*

   - *What is uncomfortable?*

   Listen reflectively and mirror back any comfort and discomfort in relationships.

2. **Introduce today's task:** establishing and maintaining healthy boundaries in relationships.

3. Review last week's homework: Ask your client to take out her Value/Action card and review together what actions she has taken so far to put her values into action. Provide positive feedback like:

   - *I like the way your actions match your values.*

   - *You did three things to make your actions match your values. Great job.*

   - *This is really moving you forward in the direction that you chose.*

   If your client struggled with this assignment, find out (in a nonjudgmental way) why. Ask what got in the way and why. Help your client identify ways in which barriers can become springboards for contemplation and further action.

4. Work on today's task: Provide psychoeducation. Here is what you can say:

   Trauma can put you into survival mode. In survival mode, you may have learned to:

   - *let whatever happens happen in order not to get hurt any further.*

   - *simply hide from others whenever possible to avoid getting hurt.*

   If you have experienced trauma, especially trauma caused by those close to you, you may be rightfully suspicious of interpersonal connections. Your experience may be that people just hurt people. Your world is now about more than past trauma. You are trying to build a meaningful life with connections. Setting healthy boundaries is a part of this life. You may feel weird or guilty about setting boundaries at first. That's OK. New things take practice. Boundaries are there to keep you safe, comfortable, *and* connected.

5. Begin by establishing the idea of body boundaries in the following way:

    - Stand opposite your client, at least four feet apart.

    - Explain that you will now walk toward your client one step at a time. After each step you will ask: Is this too close?

    - Once your client says: "Yes, this is too close," you will stop. If your client does not have a good sense of body boundaries and you get a sense that you are getting too close to her, just say: "That's close enough for me."

    Help your client reflect on this experience. Ask questions like:

    - *Are you comfortable with setting a boundary like this?*

    - *Did you know when to set the boundary?*

    - *Were you not sure about when to say "stop"?*

6. If you are working with a child, the arm's-length rule may be a good one to implement. Arm's-length is a good distance for healthy boundaries. Show your client with outstretched arms and let her show you.

7. Now, explore with your client other boundaries such as:

    - how much to reveal to a stranger or a new friend.

    - how much time and space you need to be alone.

    - "yours and mine" finances.

    - your friends and my friends.

    - stretching what is safe to do.

8. Provide psychoeducation. Say something like:

    Beware of all-or-nothing relationships in which you or your partner gives up everything. Beware of people who won't let you do your own thing. Give yourself time to tell your story to a new person. There is no rush. Maintain your own friendships and finances when you meet someone new. There is no rush to share.

    Help your client explore areas in which it is difficult for her to have clarity about boundaries. Ask:

    - *Where is it easy for you to set boundaries?*

    - *Where is it difficult?*

    Put difficulties back into the context of trauma work. You can say:

    - *It takes time to learn how to set healthy boundaries after the experience of trauma.*

- *Setting healthy boundaries can be learned.*

- *It's OK to make mistakes. Mistakes can be corrected. Mistakes just tell you that something needs to change.*

9. Review what you have done so far. You have explored how the experience of trauma can impact a sense of healthy boundaries. You have explored body boundaries and other areas in which setting boundaries can be difficult.

10. Ask your client to pick the area in which it is most important for her to set healthy boundaries right now. Write this area on an index card. Brainstorm with your client what the most important action she can take in the next few days might be. Write that action on the index card.

11. Assign homework: Ask your client to take the appropriate action chosen to maintain healthy boundaries every time the specific boundary comes up. Ask your client to use the back of the card to make a note about how she feels when maintaining healthy boundaries. Ask your client to bring the card to the next session.

12. Closing: Be sure to leave your client with words of encouragement, like:

- *Setting healthy boundaries can be learned.*

- *You are taking really important steps right now.*

- *These steps will help you feel better.*

- *Give yourself time and be patient with yourself. Setting boundaries takes practice.*

INTERVENTION 17

Being Heard and Having a Voice

The experience of trauma is very much about not having a voice and of having your voice be silenced. When there is nothing you can say to make things better, then speaking up and speaking out makes no sense. It can, in fact, make things worse. Your client may have learned to stay silent for his own protection. This intervention is meant to help your client find an assertive, clear, and courageous voice. What your client wants to say does not have to be eloquent or perfect. Speaking up is difficult. Be sure to provide positive feedback every time your client speaks up—even to you!

Target skill: Assertive communication. Taking a stand for oneself.

What you will need: It's nice to use a microphone to amplify your client's voice. Also keep ready the following index card:

Figure 56

1. Begin with empathy. Ask your client questions like:

    - *How was your week?*

    - *In what way did you stand up for yourself?*

    - *In what way did you feel you were heard?*

    - *When did you feel you were not heard?*

    Listen reflectively and mirror back to your client his experiences of success, self-efficacy, and speaking up. You can say things like:

- *It's sound to me like your last week was* [positive words client used to describe the last week] *because* [positive actions client described that created positive experiences].

- *I think you are saying that people were not listening to you.*

- *It sounds to me like you spoke up.*

- *It sounds to me like you had things to say but kept them to yourself.*

2. **Introduce today's task:** having a voice and having a say.

3. Review last week's homework. Ask your client to take out his Boundary Card and review with him which experiences went well and which did not. Ask questions like:

   - *What was it like to really think about this boundary?*

   - *Did it make a difference for you to think about this boundary?*

   - *When were you able to maintain the boundary you set?*

   - *When were you not? And what made it difficult?*

   Provide positive reinforcement for your client about beginning to be mindful of boundaries. Reiterate that this can be difficult but will become routine and comfortable over time. Also remind your client that setting healthy boundaries will help him feel and be more in control.

4. Work on today's task: Provide psychoeducation. Here is what you can say:

   Trauma can put you into survival mode. In survival mode you may have learned to:

   - *let whatever happens happen in order not to get hurt any further.*

   - *stay silent to avoid getting hurt.*

   - *simply hide from others whenever possible to avoid getting hurt.*

   If you have experienced trauma, especially trauma caused by those close to you, you may be rightfully suspicious of interpersonal connections. Your experience may be that people just hurt people and that words were mainly used to gain power and control over you.

   Your world is now about more than past trauma. You are trying to build a meaning-ful life with connections. Speaking up and making your voice heard is a part of this life. You may feel weird or guilty about speaking up at first. That's OK. New things take practice.

5. Work on today's task: Ask your client to recall a difficult situation in which he did not speak up. Help your client explore and understand the reasons for not speaking up using the following beacon to guide you:

   Is the reason you did not speak of trauma-related?

   Help your client understand that trauma can change the way we express ourselves. Even if the situation he is describing is not directly traumatic, he may still be cautious about communicating to protect himself.

6. Ask your client to tell you what he wanted to say but didn't in the difficult situation. Ask clarifying questions, and pay attention to his body language, tone, and volume. When he has finished, provide positive feedback.

7. If your client begins to apologize for what he is saying, take out the No Apologies index card. Use it with a sense of humor. You can say this:

    - *People often apologize when they have done nothing wrong. Many people do this. You are not the only one. But there is no need. You can speak up for yourself. There is nothing wrong with that.*

    - *I just want you to notice when you are over-apologizing. Is it OK if I use this card when it happens?*

    - *When you do apologize too much, there is no need to get upset about it. It's an old habit and will take time to overcome.*

8. Ask your client to try the following experiment: Give him a microphone. Ask him to, once again, tell you what he wanted to say in the difficult situation, but did not say, using the microphone. Be sure to keep the sound level appropriate (not too loud, but louder than just voice). If you do not have a microphone, you can use a toy microphone. This still emphasizes amplification.

9. Listen. Be supportive. Your client may shy away from the sound of his own amplified voice. Encourage him to simply speak and trust his voice.

10. When he is done, help him reflect on what it is like to hear his own voice amplified. Ask:

    - *What did it feel like to hear your own voice amplified?*

    - *What was your comfort level with this?*

11. Help your client reflect on what it would be like to be his own amplifier. You can say this:

    - *What would it be like to be loud and clear about what you have to say even when it is difficult?*

    - *What do you need to be able to be loud and clear?*

    Help your client reflect on his needs and how to meet them over time.

12. Ask your client to tell you once again what he wanted to say in the difficult situation, this time without the microphone. Ask him to speak loudly and clearly. Explain that you are a friendly audience. When your client is done, provide positive feedback.

13. Summarize what you have done so far. You have explored the impact trauma has had on your client's ability to make himself heard. You have experimented with amplifying your client's voice using a microphone. You have encouraged your client to be loud and clear about what he has to say even without a microphone.

14. Assign homework. Give your client the following index card. Ask your client to carry it with him and review it before he needs to speak up about some-

thing. Ask him to make note on the back of the card of situations in which he spoke up and bring the card to your next meeting.

Figure 57

15. Closing: Be sure to leave your client with words of encouragement, like:

- *Speaking up can be learned.*

- *You are taking really important steps right now.*

- *These steps will help you feel better.*

- *Give yourself time and be patient with yourself. Speaking up takes practice.*

INTERVENTION 18

Using Your Voice—Being Assertive

Trauma tells you that it is never a good idea to be assertive. Speaking up can seem pointless or dangerous. This intervention expands on the previous one. Once you have learned to use your voice, you can focus on using it in the most effective way. Many trauma survivors use a communication style that mimics the stress response: (a) They fight (verbally aggressive), (b) they verbally retreat (flight), or (c) they simply do not speak (mimicking the freeze response). This intervention will help them step out of a trauma-focused way of speaking and into an assertive use of their unique voice.

Target skill: Assertive communication.

What you will need: Paper. Writing tools. Markers and crayons. Space.

1. Begin with empathy. Welcome your client. Ask questions like:

    - *How was the last week?*

    - *When did you feel like you focused, in the way you wanted to be, on living your life the way you want to live it?*

    - *When did you feel like trauma was pulling you in the wrong direction?*

    Listen reflectively and help your client recognize ways in which she is moving away from a life that is focused on past trauma.

2. **Introduce today's task:** learning and using assertive communication. Review last week's homework. Ask questions like:

    - *When did you use your Loud and Clear index card?*

    - *What was the situation?*

    - *Were you able to find your voice, loud and clear?*

    - *Were there difficulties with this?*

    Again, provide positive feedback for any steps your client took toward making her voice heard. Reassure your client that perfection is not needed. She is taking steps in the right direction, and over time speaking up will become easier.

3. Work on today's task: understanding and learning assertive communication. Provide psychoeducation. You can say:

    - *Trauma can put you into survival mode. In survival mode you may have learned to:*

        - *let whatever happens happen in order not to get hurt any further.*

        - *stay silent to avoid getting hurt.*

        - *simply hide from others whenever possible to avoid getting hurt.*

    - *If you have experienced trauma, especially trauma caused by those close to you, you may be rightfully suspicious of interpersonal connections. Your expe-*

*rience may be that people just hurt people and that words were mainly used
to gain power and control over you.*

- *Your world is now about more than past trauma. You are trying to build a
meaningful life with connections. Speaking up and becoming assertive is part
of this life. You may feel weird or guilty about becoming assertive at first.
That's OK. New things take practice.*

4. Explore different communication styles. You can show your client the following image:

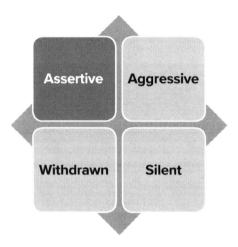

Figure 58

Help your client explore and understand how these different communication styles can relate to traumatic experiences. You can say:

Trauma puts you into survival mode. In survival mode you might

- *use an aggressive tone of voice and harsh words to defend yourself. People
do this because they do not want to get hurt. This is the equivalent of the fight
response.*

- *be quiet and not contradict anyone, or use a quiet tone of voice. People use
this withdrawn communication style because they do not want to get hurt.
This is the equivalent of a flight response.*

- *simply not speak. People do this with the hope that it will help them avoid
getting hurt. This is the equivalent of the freeze response.*

5. Use the image above to help your client explore what her communication
styles are (they are likely to vary at different times, in different places, and
with different people). You can ask:

- *When do you tend to be loud and use angry words?*

- *When do you tend to say very little?*

- *When are you simply silent?*

Help your client explore and understand how her ways of communicating may have served a protective role in the past but may no longer be the best fit.

6. Suggest that there's another way of communicating: being assertive. Explain that assertiveness is:

    - saying what you have to say.

    - saying it clearly.

    - saying it in a way that the recipient can receive it.

    - free of insults and attacks.

    - not apologetic about taking a stand.

    Also explain that assertive communication is the best way to get one's needs met in a situation that is not dangerous.

7. Summarize what you have done so far. You have learned about assertive communication, explored reasons for not being assertive, and discovered how those reasons can be trauma-related.

8. Assign homework: Ask your client to pick a common situation in which it would help her to be assertive. Explore the situation with her (make sure that the situation presents no danger) and help her write an assertive paragraph related to this situation on an index card. Ask her to carry the index card with her and read it out loud every day. Then ask her to try to use an assertive communication style when the situation appears.

9. Closing: Be sure to leave your client with words of encouragement. You can say:

    - *Being assertive can help you be true to yourself.*

    - *You are taking steps to be true to yourself.*

    - *This can feel tricky at first.*

    - *Just practice. Don't worry about perfection.*

Affect Regulation Interventions

When stressful things happen, our body has a mechanism to respond to them. In stressful situations, our central nervous system "fires up" so that we can be ready to fight (or run) for our survival. When our clients are in survival mode—and many still are when they arrive in therapy—managing feelings is not on the forefront of their minds because biology dictates that it not be a priority. For those of our clients who have grown up under conditions of toxic stress and ongoing developmental trauma, affect regulation may be especially difficult because:

- They never learned to recognize their feelings.
- They never learned why feelings might be important.
- They may only know basic feelings such as happiness, sadness, anger, and rage.
- They may not be able to understand whether they are angry or sad.
- Happiness and joy may feel strange and create a sense that something is wrong.

While it is beyond the scope of this manual to create a full list of affect regulation interventions, the following interventions are designed to address the very basic issues of understanding what feelings are and what they are for, and learning to turn the volume of a feeling up or down, depending on the situation.

INTERVENTION 19

Welcome to Your Feelings—They Are Here to Help

The following intervention is designed to give your client a basic understanding of what feelings are, where they come from, and what their function might be. Additionally, your client will learn that feelings are not necessarily "true," meaning that while they may be present, they may not relate well to the situation.

Target skill: Recognizing feelings and their function in context.

What you will need: Paper. Index cards. Drawing and writing tools.

1. Begin with empathy. Check in with your client. Ask questions like:

    - *How was the last week?*

    - *How connected did you feel with yourself?*

    - *What did you do to feel alive?*

    - *When did you speak up for yourself?*

    Listen reflectively and help your client "own" any areas in which he has made progress.

2. **Introduce today's task:** learning about feelings and their function.

3. Review last week's homework. Ask questions like:

    - *Did you carry your assertiveness index card with you and read it once every day?*

    - *When did you give assertiveness a try?*

    - *How did you feel when you tried?*

    - *What went well? What did not?*

    Be sure to give your client positive feedback about any attempts to be assertive. If your client did not try in a real situation, check if he read the card out loud to himself daily. This alone can be progress.

4. Work on today's task. You can say this:

    When traumatic and stressful things happen, our body tells us to run, hide, or fight. These three things are all body-related and require immediate action. It is not helpful to feel sad when you are being chased by a tiger. All energy must go to ensuring survival. If you have grown up with a lot of stress and trauma, you may never have been able to pay much attention to how you feel. You may not understand what feelings are and how they can be useful. You may even perceive them as threatening.

    There are many ways in which feelings can be useful:

    - *They can tell us that something is wrong.*

    - *They can call us into action.*

    - *They can connect us with others.*

    - *They can give us a sense of safety or danger.*

Here is something that can be tricky about feelings: Just because you have a feeling does not mean that the feeling relates to what is going on in the moment. Old feelings can pop up. Here is an example:

Sara has a bad feeling about her new boss. She feels afraid of him and has the need to run out of the office. She later realizes that he wore an aftershave that reminded her of the one her fiancé wore when he assaulted her.

When feelings pop up, it can be useful to notice them and examine them. They do not always need to be acted upon, especially when they do not relate to the current context.

5. Ask your client to recall a recent situation in which he became very upset. Then help him reflect on the situation, asking questions like:

   - *What was the situation?*
   - *What feeling came up quickly?*
   - *How intense was the feeling?*
   - *In what way did the feeling relate to the current situation?*
   - *In what way did the feeling relate to or remind you of other past/traumatic situations?*
   - *Thinking about this now, do you think it would have been helpful to be able to step back and examine the feeling for a moment?*
   - *Do you think it would have been helpful to be able to turn the volume of the feeling up or down?*

6. Map these steps using the following diagram:

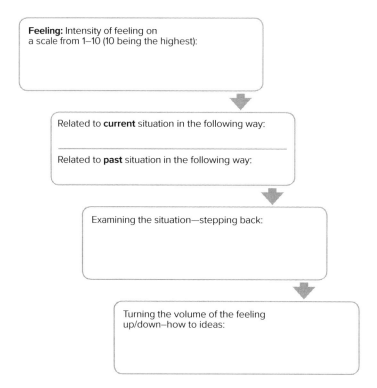

Figure 59

7. Once you have completed all the steps, ask: *What new things have you learned about feelings and how they work?* Be sure to reiterate that feelings are not "good" or "bad." They just are. They can be helpful, but sometimes they need to be examined and managed.

8. Summarize what you have done so far. You have learned to understand feelings and their usefulness. You have learned how trauma can impact the way you relate to feelings. You have learned to examine feelings.

9. Assign homework. Give your client a copy of the Feelings Diagram to take home. Ask him to pick a difficult situation that led to an intense feeling and then examine this feeling using the above diagram. He should complete each part of the diagram. Ask him to bring the diagram back to your next meeting.

10. Closing: Be sure to send your client home with words of encouragement. You can say:

    - *You are learning to examine your feelings.*

    - *This may be new to you.*

    - *It's OK to struggle with this.*

    - *Being able to examine and relate to your feelings in new ways can be very helpful with living a life that is not focused on past trauma.*

INTERVENTION 20

When Feelings Are Overwhelming

For trauma survivors, feelings can become overwhelming fast. The very experience of having a feeling can be perceived as a threat, and so they may have learned to "turn off" or "put away" their feelings. Of course, neither of those choices tends to work out over time. Feelings linger or fester, demanding attention. This intervention is designed to help your client accept and explore a difficult feeling. Keep in mind that this may be an altogether new experience for her.

Target skill: Acceptance of feelings. Defusion from overwhelming feelings.

What you will need: Paper. Writing and drawing tools. Index cards.

1. Begin with empathy. Check in with your client. Ask questions like:

    - *How was the last week?*

    - *How connected did you feel with yourself?*

    - *What did you do to feel alive?*

    - *In what way did you attend to your feelings? In what way did you not?*

    Listen reflectively and help your client "own" any areas in which she has made progress.

2. **Introduce today's task:** recognizing and working with overwhelming feelings. Review last week's homework. Ask:

    How did you use your feelings diagram?

    Take a look at the feelings diagram together. Was your client able to explore in what ways her feelings were connected to the past and the present? Was she able to step back from her feeling without disregarding it? What did your client do to "turn down" the intensity of her feelings?

    Be sure to give your client positive feedback about any attempts to understand and manage her feelings. If your client was able to step back and gain some distance from her feeling, this is a success!

3. Work on today's task: Provide psychoeducation. You can say this:

    Many of us have been taught that we should pay attention to and honor our feelings. This is mostly good advice. Feelings, however, can show up in odd places, at odd times. They can show up out of context. Many trauma survivors are familiar with this experience.

    You may be somewhere safe, but all of a sudden you feel unsafe, threatened, and panicked because something in the environment triggered an emotional response related to past trauma.

    It can be useful to learn to manage feelings by attending to them without getting attached to them. When you get attached to a feeling, you just run with it. You believe the feeling and act immediately. When you attend to the feeling, you recognize it and honor it, but you do not act on it impulsively. You may sit with it and talk to it to see what needs to happen to it. This process tends to turn down the intensity of the feeling.

4. Ask your client to think about a situation in which she had a difficult feeling, but not the most difficult feeling she has ever had. Ask her to recall that feeling and describe the feeling to you by:

    - naming the feeling.

    - naming the demands it makes, and speculating on the feeling.

    - naming the actions she would take if she gave in to those demands impulsively.

5. Help your client examine the impact of listening to and impulsively following the demands of a feeling. Help your client name the outcome of impulsively listening to her feelings. You can ask your client to complete the following sentence:

    If I had done what this feeling had told me, then _____ _____ would have happened.

6. Help your client explore and understand if the outcome she is describing is in line with her values. The idea is to get some distance between your client and an impulsive response to a feeling.

7. You can use the following image to help your client explore how she can gain some distance to a feeling:

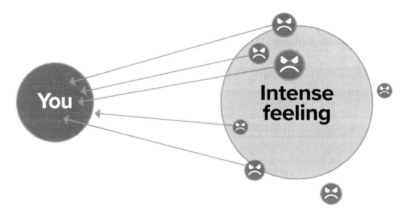

Figure 60

8. You can say:

    There you are. Your intense feeling is sending you a lot of urgent messages. It's kind of like being bombarded. Let's try to take a step back from the big, intense feeling. You can still feel it, but you are stepping back. You are not attached to it or fused to it. It is just there.

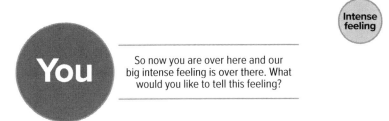

Figure 61

9. Ask your client to develop a conversation with the big, intense feeling. You, the therapist, can play the part of the feeling, like:

> Big Intense Feeling: *You, right there. Listen to me. Hey, listen. Yes, you. You gotta do this. You have to get that guy and you have to get him good. Do it now. Have it over with once and for all.*

> Therapist (as client): *Hello there, big intense feeling. You are a bit much right now. You are like a big roaring dragon. Wow. That is impressive. Let me take a look at you.*

> Big Intense Feeling: *No time to look, no time. Do it. Do it now. Get the guy. Why are you still sitting here?*

> Therapist (as client): *I am just wondering about you. Part of me wants to listen to you, and part of me thinks you are overdoing it. I get why you are so big and intense. But what you are suggesting just won't work. Here is what I can do: I will listen to you to make you feel better, but I will not run and do what you tell me to do.*

> You get the idea. You want your client to defuse (separate from her big intense feeling without disregarding it).

10. When you are done role playing, help your client identify what may help her in her daily life to separate from her feelings without disregarding them. Make a list on an index card.

**Steps to take to separate
from a big, intense feeling:**

1. Greet the feeling.

2. Name the feeling.

3. Welcome the feeling.

4. Do the following to gain distance from the feeling:

   • _____

   • _____

   • _____

   • _____

Figure 62

11. Summarize what you have done so far: You have explored together how feelings can get intense and demand to take over. You have explored how to talk to an intense feeling and made a plan how to respond to it without disregarding it.

12. Assign homework: Ask your client to take the Big Intense Feeling card home and use it when the next big intense feeling comes along. Ask your client to use the back of the index card to make a note of how her response to the big intense feeling went. What worked and what did not work?

13. Closing: Be sure to send your client home with words of encouragement, like:

    • *Big intense feelings can be bothersome.*

    • *But they don't need to be.*

    • *You can talk to them.*

    • *You can even be friendly to them.*

    • *You don't have to do what they tell you.*

Resource Building Interventions

When your client is in survival mode, anything nonessential to survival takes a back seat. This includes connecting with others and with resources that could make things better. All energy moves into actions that support survival. At the end of the day your client is just exhausted. There is no time or mental energy left to look for the things he needs.

Yet, in order to get better, trauma survivors need access to resources such as:

- a peer support group, such as NAMI;
- a way to experience joy through connection;
- access to basic resources, such as housing, food, clothing;
- support for gaining and maintaining meaningful employment;
- access to other services that wrap around their needs, such as psychiatric services, support for SUD.

This, of course, is not a comprehensive list. When your client needs these kinds of resources and supports, refer him to a case manager such as a therapeutic behavioral services provider. You and the case manager (TBS provider) will need to work together on establishing a hierarchy of needs. If your client is homeless, this needs to be addressed first. It is not unusual for trauma survivors to have very unstable lives. It is also not unusual for trauma survivors to have stable lives (and a lot of emotional pain). Find out where your client falls on this spectrum.

If your client cannot gain access to case management or other supportive services, you should explore with him other ways in which his resource needs can be met. You, the therapist, can also provide some of these kinds of supports by providing case management services. You should discuss with your supervisor how much of this you should do to avoid role confusion.

The following interventions address resource building from a therapeutic point of view. They are meant to help your client explore and understand the need to look for and accept all kinds of help.

INTERVENTION 21

All by Myself

This intervention is designed to help your client explore and understand the need to seek out and accept help.

Target skill: Seeking and accepting help

What you will need: Small suitcase or any kind of small bag. Individual index cards saying:

- Housing
- Food
- Clothing
- Support group
- Medicine
- Education
- Substance Use Services
- Childcare
- Employment
- Friends
- Furniture

Add as many things as needed and place these cards in a small box on the table.

1. Welcome your client. Begin with empathy. Ask questions like:

    - *How did your week go?*
    - *Who did you connect with?*
    - *What was missing from your life?*
    - *Were there any urgent needs?*

2. **Introduce today's task:** seeking out and accepting resources.

3. Review last week's homework. Ask questions like:

    - *In what way did you use your Big Intense Feelings card?*
    - *Which steps on the card were useful to you?*
    - *How did your relationship with the big intense feeling change after using the card?*

    Provide positive feedback for any small step taken. Just using the card means that your client has tried to step back from the big intense feeling.

4. Work on today's task: moving from *All by myself* to *Finding help together*. Provide psychoeducation. You can say this:

Trauma often tells you that you are all alone. Many trauma survivors feel that they can't trust anyone and that they really should be able to do everything by themselves. The truth is that no one can do everything by themselves. We all depend on each other. Needing help is not a personal fault, but rather a human condition.

Ask your client how she feels about needing help.

- How does she think about herself?

- Is it difficult to admit that help is needed?

- What messages does trauma send her about needing help?

- How does she relate to those messages?

5. Once you have explored your client's feelings about needing and accepting help, ask her to engage in the following exercise:

   Put the box of index cards indicating various needs on the table. Also put a small suitcase or backpack there. Then ask your client to draw cards out of the box one by one. If she feels she needs resources in the area of need picked, she should put the card in the suitcase. If she feels she does not, she can put the card aside.

6. Once your client has drawn all the cards, take a look at the cards in the suitcase/backpack. These are the areas in which your client needs resources. Introduce the idea of a referral to a worker who can help with resources.

7. Explore with your client possible reluctance to accepting a referral to a worker who can assist with resources. You can ask:

   - *Will it be tricky to meet and trust a new person?*

   - *Do you feel like you should not need this help?*

   - *Do you feel unworthy of the help?*

   - *Do you feel that you can do this alone?*

   Explore reluctance to accept help in a kind manner. If your client feels that she can do it all alone, one response you can give is:

   Yes, you can. But it would probably take much longer and be exhausting. It's not that you can't do it. It's that part of your job right now is to learn to accept help and even accept that others can be helpful and can be trusted.

   Of course, if your client truly does not need any additional resources, then there is no need to push them on her.

8. Summarize what you have done so far. You have explored the idea that trauma can push people into isolation and that this isolation can lead to a lack of resources. You have also explored how a lack of resources can impede recovery from trauma. Your client has explored how she feels about accepting help and what kinds of resources she needs.

9. Assign homework: Ask your client to pick one of the cards indicating a resource need, but not the one with the greatest need. Ask her to take the card home and, over the next week, specify on the back of the card the ways her need could be met.

10. Closing: Be sure to leave your client with words of encouragement, like:

- *It's OK to seek help. We all need help.*

- *There are people who want to help.*

- *Trusting others is a great step!*

INTERVENTION 22

Taking a Chance

This intervention is designed to help your client explore past experiences of broken trust and then move into mindful trusting of other for help.

Target skill: Mindful trust. Accepting help.

What you will need: Paper. Writing and drawing tools. Index cards.

1. Begin with empathy. Check in with your client by asking questions like:

   - How did the last week go?

   - In what way did someone help you?

   - How did you feel when someone offered help?

2. **Introduce today's task:** mindfully accepting help.

3. Review last week's homework. Ask your client to take out the "needs" index card.

   - What needs did he specify on the back?

   - What were his ideas about getting these needs met?

   - Are there any concrete steps he can take?

   - Who does he need to talk to? Where does he need to go?

   Any thoughts your client put into specifying needs should be praised. He is considering the idea that he needs resources and that needs can be met. This is a very different mindset from feeling overwhelmed and withdrawing.

4. Work on today's task: Provide psychoeducation. You can say:

   Trauma can take away your ability to trust others. People you trusted have hurt you. Your experience has been that others bring you pain. But just like people can hurt each other, people can also heal and help each other. We need to build an experience of trust and help from another person that is safe. Once you have this experience, it may be easier for you to mindfully trust others.

5. Ask your client to explore a past experience during which his trust was broken. Ask questions like:

   - *What happened?*

   - *What was this person going to do for you?*

   - *What did you know about this person?*

   - *How did they break your trust?*

6. Help your client differentiate between mindful and impulsive trust. You can use the following image to help with this:

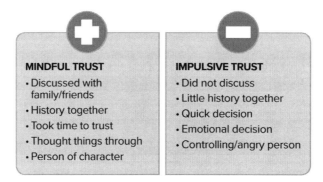

Figure 63

7. Help your client reflect on his past negative experience. Ask questions like:

    - *Did you discuss trusting this person with family and friends?*

    - *How long did you know this person?*

    - *How much time did you take to decide to trust this person?*

    - *Did you think things through?*

    - *How much did you know about this person's character?*

    Be sure to reiterate: When someone else hurts you, it is not your fault. It is their fault. The goal of examining past experiences is to build a better experience for the future.

8. Ask your client to pick a resource need, but not the greatest need. Then ask him to pick a person who may be able to meet the need and examine with you if this person can be trusted, using the chart above.

9. Summarize what you have done so far: Your client has explored the connection between trauma and broken trust. Your client has learned about mindful vs. impulsive trust and has explored a past experience of broken trust using these measures.

10. Assign homework: Send your client home with this image on an index card:

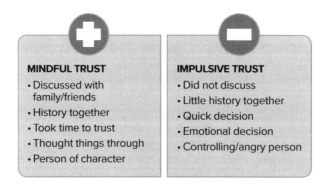

Figure 64

Ask your client to approach the person he picked and express his resource need, then ask for help with this need. Ask your client to record his experience with this person on the back of the card, then bring the card to the next meeting.

11. Closing: End the session with words of encouragement, like:

- *Trust can be built.*

- *Trust can be examined.*

- *You can learn to mindfully trust others.*

- *There is help.*

- *And you can find this help.*

INTERVENTION 23

The Best of All Worlds

This intervention is about dreaming. What would your client's life be like if she had all the resources she needed and wanted? Once you have identified the resources your client needs and wants (and could get if she had a magic wand), you can then move into understanding where to start with what is realistic.

Target skill: Thinking big. Being practical.

What you will need: Paper. Writing and drawing tools. Index cards

1. Begin with empathy. Ask your client questions like:

   - *How was the last week?*

   - *What went well?*

   - *Who did you trust?*

   - *Who could you not trust?*

   Be sure to provide positive feedback to your client regarding any steps she took toward feeling connected and beginning to trust mindfully.

2. **Introduce today's task:** creating an image of the best of all worlds, in terms of resources, and then bringing it "down to earth" and making it real.

3. Review last week's homework. Ask questions like:

   - *Were you able to approach the person you picked and talk with this person about helping with resources?*

   - *How did you feel asking?*

   - *How did it go?*

   - *How did the person respond?*

   - *Do you think the person you picked was trustworthy? If yes, then why? If not, then why not?*

4. Work on today's task: Provide psychoeducation. You can say this:

   People who have experienced trauma often feel like the things they need now should just be given to them. This is understandable. Trauma can rob you of material things but also emotional resources, your physical health, and your relationships. Dreaming about resources can be a good thing. What would magically appear if you could have all resources in the world? What would be the first thing to appear? Once you have let yourself dream, it is equally important to bring things down to earth and to make real the things that can be real.

5. Begin by asking your client to dream of all the resources she would need to heal from her traumatic experience if there were no restrictions. She can either draw or write. Resources can be all kinds of things:

   - people

   - food

- furniture
- medical care
- access to mental health care
- housing
- finances
- animals
- for children: things like dolls, Legos, and game systems may come up.

6. Once your client has created an image/list, bring it down to the here and now by asking:

    - *Which of these things is most important to you?*

    - *And which of these things could really happen?*

7. Help your client explore and understand the differences between what should happen (things should appear to a trauma survivor just out of fairness) and the reality of building one's resources one by one. Ask your client:

    What is the difference between asking "Why do I have to make this happen?" and "How do I feel about being able to take control of what I need?"

    Spend time exploring this tension between wanting to be taken care of and taking control of one's own needs. Validate the need to feel and be taken care of and the reality of being in charge of one's own life.

8. Review what you have done so far: Your client has dreamed about unlimited resources. You have explored the tension between wanting to be taken care of (unlimited resources) and the reality of being in charge of one's own life. Your client has identified which resource is most important to her and which could truly become a part of her life.

9. Assign homework: Give your client an index card naming the resource that is most important for her to build. Ask her to use the back of the card to identify resources available to her right now that could meet some of her needs in some way. You can explain that using imperfect resources is better than not using resources at all. Ask her to bring this card to your next meeting.

10. Closing: Be sure to leave your client with words of encouragement, like:

    - *It's OK to dream.*

    - *It's good to make dreams as real as possible.*

    - *You can build your own resources with the help of others.*

Interventions for Communicating Trauma Experiences

In many ways traumatic experiences can be a silencer. Because traumatic experiences, by definition, fall out of ordinary experience, they are difficult to communicate. Traumatic experiences can force us to question everything that we hold dear: our faith in others, our sense of safety, our trust that those around us mean well. The shock can render us speechless. Traumatic experiences can be stuck in wordless terror.

Finding words and other ways of communicating traumatic experiences can be crucial to recovery. Once an experience is communicated, your client is no longer fully alone with it. Your client is now in connection with another human being. Trauma breaks connections. Empathy and language rebuild those connections.

How clients tell their trauma stories can greatly vary. Sometimes there is an assumption that the details of the traumatic experience must be recounted. This is not necessarily true. Neither is the idea that once the story is told, the telling of the story is complete. Trauma is processed over time. A child will tell his story in one way, then tell it differently twenty years later.

But the initial telling can help your client contain the traumatic experience and send him into connection with others. Sharing can lead to hope that one is not completely alone. While telling his story, your client can also begin to accept that the traumatic experience is now over. It is present in the telling of the story, but the experience is in the past.

Be sure that your client has a substantial number of coping skills mastered before helping him tell his story. It is important that your client be able to manage intense feelings that come up in the process.

How can the story be told? You can certainly ask, carefully, if your client is ready. Then listen with care. If your client can't find the words, it's OK to ask if he needs help. Express an understanding that words are just an approximation of what he has to say.

Pay attention to your client's affect. How is his breathing? Can he make eye contact? Is he so overwhelmed by emotion that he begins to dissociate? If this is the case, help your client ground himself back in the here and now using a powerful sensory experience such as biting into an orange or opening a window and letting the air flow in. If your client is dissociative, telling the story can be re-traumatizing. Grounding him in the present is essential.

A child or creative adult may want to use nonverbal ways of communicating his traumatic experience. This is OK. Give your client the time and freedom he needs to tell his story in his own way. If the story is told visually, ask, "What do I see here?" to help your client add language to his story. You want him to experience sharing what was previously a lonely and terrifying experience.

If your client wrote a story or a poem about his traumatic experience, ask him to read it to you. You can offer to read the story to him when he is done. If your client wrote a song, ask him to sing it to you, then see if you can sing it together. Again, the emphasis is on overcoming terrifying aloneness in a terrifying story.

What if the story very short, and you know from another source that there is a lot more to tell? This is OK. Some trauma survivors tell their stories in detail; some do not. One is not better than the other as long as the story gets told.

Many trauma survivors have recounted the details of their story many times—to the police, the court, their friends, etc.—and may now tell it without emotion, almost as if talking about someone else. Pay attention to your client's affect. Is your client able to connect to his feelings while telling the story without being overwhelmed by them? Can your client make eye contact with you, or is his gaze glassy or distant? The telling of the story is only helpful for your client if he is present. If he is not, go back to helping him ground himself in the here and now using a strong sensory experience.

The following interventions are designed to help your client tell his story. Remember: Skills first! Be sure that your client has the self-soothing and grounding skills he needs to tell his story.

INTERVENTION 24

Sharing the Hurt

This intervention is designed to help your client tell her story using words. You will need to be ready to hear the story in as much or as little detail as your client will use. Listening to traumatic stories can be difficult. You should be able to listen empathically. You should not interject your own interpretations or say things that will detract from the truth of your client's story.

If your client can dissociate from her story and her feelings about it, so can you. If you put too much distance between your client's story and you, then the story is no longer being shared. Your client will notice. Be present and open up to your client's story.

Target skill: Creating and containing traumatic experiences in a story. Sharing the story. Being the author of one's own story.

What you will need: Just your ability to listen empathically. Keep pen and paper ready in case you or your client want to take notes. Tissues. Index card. Small box.

1. Begin with empathy. Ask questions like:

    - *How was your week?*

    - *Who did you connect with this week?*

    - *When did you feel really connected this week?*

    - *When did you feel alone?*

    Listen for moments of ability to connect and help your client recognize those moments and her ability to connect in spite of her trauma.

2. Introduce today's task: sharing the story of hurt and creating healing in the process.

3. Review last week's homework. Ask your client to take out her resource card. Together take a look at the front of the card. Which resource is most important to your client? Give your client positive feedback for her ability to know what she needs. Then ask her to turn the card over. What steps did she identify to obtain it? Go over the steps with her, then identify with her what she can do in the following week to get closer to meeting her resource need. Be sure to give your client positive feedback for bringing things down to earth and identifying concrete steps.

    If your client did not write anything on the back of the card, ask what got in the way. Then model for your client how to make things concrete. Here is an example:

    Your client's identified resource need is her own house. Your client is currently homeless and living in a shelter with her children.

    - Bringing it down to earth: looking for subsidized housing, perhaps an apartment to start with.

- Making it real: filling out an application for public housing. Looking at apartment listings to see what is available.

4. Work on today's task: Provide psychoeducation. You can say this:

> *It's important to tell your story when you are ready. Before sharing it, you should have a solid set of skills to manage your feelings related to your trauma story so that you aren't overwhelmed by intense feelings. It can be difficult to find words. This is OK. Your words do not have to be perfect. You can tell the complete story with as much detail as you want, or you can summarize in any way you need to. Both of these ways of telling the story are OK.*

> *I will be here with you and listen. In this way you are no longer alone with your story. You will have told it and connected with another human being. You will have found a way to contain it in words. It will become part of the past. It is present in the telling, but it is a part of your past that is told, shared, and contained.*

5. Ask your client to tell her story. You can facilitate this by asking questions like:

- *How does your story begin? Was there a time when all was well?*
- *What changed? When did the hurt begin? Was it sudden or did you get hurt more and more over time?*
- *Who or what hurt you?*
- *If your hurt came from a person, who was this person to you? Were they close to you or a stranger?*
- *What kind of hurt was it? Were you injured?*
- *Was there anyone who helped you?*
- *Were you able to help yourself in any way?*
- *How did you feel?*
- *When did the hurt end, and how did it end?*
- *When and how did you know you were safe?*
- *What helped you survive?*

Listen to your client's story empathically. Do not interrupt. If your client has questions, answer them. If your client needs reassurance about telling her story, provide it. If your client expresses worry about hurting you by telling you the story, tell her that you are able to listen, that you value her story, and that you believe that humans heal in connection with each other. If your client is crying, provide tissues and emotional support. Reassure your client that crying is OK. It is an expression of connecting with her feelings.

6. Once your client has concluded, thank her for telling her story. You can say:

- *Thank you for sharing your story.*

- *I am honored that you trusted me with your story.*

- *You have done well telling your story. You have found words to say the unspeakable.*

- *In this way you have contained your story.*

7. Help your client identify a way in which, symbolically, she can put her story away. Perhaps your client needs to "leave" her story with you for the next week. You can write her name on an index card and offer to put the card—representing her story—in a small box. Or she can take the box with her.

8. Summarize what you have done so far: Your client has explored how telling the story of her traumatic experience can be helpful. She has told her story of hurt, and you have shared the experience with her. She has become the author of her own story and symbolically contained it.

9. Assign homework: Many trauma survivors report that the story invades their everyday lives. Ask your client to identify three ways in which she can contain her story when she wants to. Give your client an index card to record this and ask her to bring the card back to your next meeting.

10. Closing: Send your client home with words of connection. You can say:

- *Sharing your story was courageous.*

- *You carry your story with you, but it is in the past.*

- *You contained your story.*

- *You can choose to look at your story as needed and you can choose to put your story away as needed.*

INTERVENTION 25

Working on Containment

Your client has learned to share his story in a safe environment. This signals an ability to contain. The therapeutic relationships serve as a holding environment for the difficult story. The therapist helps the client regulate and co-regulate as needed. But, of course, containment has to happen outside of the therapeutic environment and relationship. This intervention is designed to help your client identify and use several ways of containing the story of trauma when it needs to be contained.

Target skill: Containment. Emotion regulation.

What you will need: Paper. Writing tools. Stapler. Box or basket.

1. Begin with empathy. Ask your client questions like:

   - *How did the week go?*

   - *Now that you have told your story, how do you feel?*

   - *When did you think about the experience of telling your story?*

   - *What was it like to think about the experience of telling your story?*

   Listen reflectively and provide positive feedback about your client's ability to explore and think about his story. The simple act of doing so already symbolizes his ability to step back and defuse from his story.

2. **Introduce today's task:** containing the trauma story and related difficult feelings.

3. Review last week's homework. Ask your client about last week's experiences of opening up about and containing his story. You can ask:

   - *When did you share parts of your story?*

   - *What was the experience like?*

   - *How were you able to put the story away when needed?*

   - *If you did not share, which is perfectly fine, how did you think about your story during the week? How were you able to put the story away when this was needed?*

4. Work on today's task: Provide psychoeducation. You can say this:

   Many trauma survivors struggle with the process of opening up about their story and then putting the story away. This is because strong emotional reactions can be involved. It is best to have an assortment of containment strategies at the ready.

5. Help your client explore different ways of containing the story. Be sure to explore what may work for your client in his context. Here are some ideas:

   - Mentally (or symbolically) putting the story in a box/drawer.

   - Writing a summary of the story in a book. Choosing when to open and close as well as put away the book.

- Holding the story with compassion in your hands, then "tucking it in" under a blanket.

- Sending the story on vacation and planning for its return.

Note that these are just examples. All of these means of containment can be done in your client's mind or acted out as a ritual of containment.

6. Once your client has picked/developed a containment activity, make this activity as specific as possible by writing out a script. Use words of containment like:

    - *Care, kindness, and compassion.*

    - *Safe and sound.*

    - *Held.*

    - *The story waits its turn.*

7. Here is an example of the process: Your client has chosen to write his story in a book. It's easy to make a simple booklet out of paper using a stapler.

    - Ask your client to write his name on the outside followed by the word "story."

    - Then ask your client to write his story in the book. The pages can become sections of the story. Your client can choose to write a summary or a detailed account. Your client can also choose to illustrate it any way he wants to.

    - Once the story is finished, explore with your client the opening and closing of the book. Explain that this closing symbolizes the containment of the story. It is his story, and he can choose to look at it and choose to put it away.

    - Make plans to keep the book safe (another metaphor for containment). Where will your client put the book? Does it need to be locked away? Can he put it on a shelf?

8. Summarize what you have done so far: Your client has explored the importance of containing his story and created or picked a method for doing so.

9. Assign homework: Ask your client to practice opening and closing his story. Once a day he should take a few minutes to think about his story with kindness, then put it away. You can explain that like everything else, contain-

ment takes practice. Give your client the following homework chart to check off completion of the assignment and bring it back to your next meeting:

Opening and closing the story:
Monday:
Tuesday:
Wednesday:
Thursday:
Friday:
Saturday:
Sunday:

Figure 65

10. Closing: Send your client home with words of encouragement. You can say:

- Containing your story becomes easier over time and with practice.

- You can be kind to yourself and your story.

INTERVENTION 26

Protecting Your Story

When trauma survivors share their stories, inevitably, there will be attempts at intrusion into the story. Many of these attempts are well intentioned, though not helpful. Other attempts at intrusion are motivated by a sense of sensationalist narcissism. The person listening may find the story interesting but have no empathy for the survivor. The following intervention is designed to help your client begin the task of protecting her story from unwanted and unhelpful intrusions.

Target skill: Taking charge of one's story. Boundary setting.

What you will need: Index cards and writing tools. Laminator or tape.

1. Begin with empathy. Ask your client questions like:

    *   *How was the week?*

    *   *In what way was your story with you?*

    *   *How did you feel about your story?*

    Listen reflectively and highlight your client's ability to differentiate between herself and her story.

2. **Introduce today's task:** protecting one's story.

3. Review last week's homework. Take a look at your client's homework chart together. Ask questions like:

    *   *In what way were you able to practice opening and closing your story every day?*

    *   *How easy/difficult was this?*

    *   *What was particularly effective? What did not work?*

    Explore with your client the idea that learning to contain the story is an ongoing process. Also explain that containing the story does not refer to suppressing feelings related to the story. It just means being able to let go of those feelings when it is time.

4. Work on today's task: Provide psychoeducation. You can say:

    *   *Many trauma survivors have noticed attempts at intrusion into their story. Many of these attempts are well intentioned, though not helpful. Perhaps someone may give you advice on how to better handle your situation. Or someone may point out some sort of important life lesson your story should have taught you. Again, well intentioned, but not helpful.*

    *   *Other attempts at intrusion are motivated by a sense of sensationalism. These attempts may be disguised as interest, but you may notice that this person is feeding on your story. The person listening may not be interested in the story being your story, but rather in absorbing the story and its gory details for themselves. They find the story interesting but have no in interest you. The following intervention is designed to help you keep ownership of the story and*

*find ways of setting boundaries about sharing the story. It is, after all, yours.
You own it.*

5. Present your client with the following scenarios one after the other.

- Scenario 1: An acquaintance approaches you. She has just found out about your traumatic experience and wants to help. She immediately hugs you. Then she says: "I feel so sorry for you. It's just terrible that this happened. The next time you are in this kind of situation you should really (insert advice). But at least you learned (insert life lesson). I know this woman you should talk to. How about next Wednesday? I will take you there. OK, it's set then. She does aromatherapy and it works wonders."

- Scenario 2: One of your colleagues at work approaches you. He is the guy who is always first on the scene when something interesting happens, and he wants to know all the details no matter what,. He often revels in describing situations that have nothing to do with him. He approaches you and says: "Hi there, sweetie. I hear this thing happened to you. Tell me all about it. I think it is so important for you to share. It will make you feel better. I am here to listen. You can call me any time day and night to talk." When you thank him and try to walk away (because you know this guy), he puts his hand on your shoulder and says: "Many experts agree that it is important to share. Not sharing can result in long-term problems. Are you sure you don't want to take advantage of this opportunity, sweetie?"

6. Take out at least two index cards and help your client develop appropriate and boundary-setting responses to both of these situations. You may want to ask:

What is your first response to each situation? If you were to not think about the situation, what would you say (and how would you feel)? Give your client a chance to express this emotional reaction to you. It's OK to have strong emotions about this.

These strong emotions will then inform the response your client will prepare for these kinds of situations.

Help your client extract from the emotional response the content of what really needs to be said. Here are some things that may come up:

- No one can tell me what I am thinking or feeling.

- It's my story. I decide when and how to share.

- Don't assume that you know my situation.

- Don't assume that you know better.

- Don't tell me what I should have done. This implies that I could have gotten out of the situation, that somehow this is my fault.

- Don't tell me that you know what will help. You don't.

- Don't try to take over. It's insulting. I am an adult.

- Your interest in my traumatic experience is borderline creepy. I don't normally tell you about my life, so I won't tell you about my trauma.

- Don't stand so close to me. Don't touch me.

7. Take out index card one and prepare a response for scenario one. The response should be short and concise, no more than three to four sentences. It's best to keep the response nonemotional. Your client's goal is to let go of the situation and not get into a debate.

What to say to someone who is trying to be helpful but really does not understand:

1. I understand you are trying to help,

2. but _____ ,

3. and _____ ,

4. so, _____ .

Figure 66

8. Take out index card two and prepare a response for scenario two. The response should be short and concise, no more than three to four sentences. It's best to keep the response nonemotional. Your client's goal is to let go of the situation and not get into a debate.

**What to say to someone who
is intrusive and uncaring:**

5. This is not your business.

6. I am asking you to _____ .

7. I need you to quit _____ .

8. Otherwise I may have to _____ .

Figure 67

9. Once your client has completed those two cards, practice with her how to use the cards in role play. It's OK if the role-playing becomes humorous. You should explain that it's important to practice the responses so that they come naturally when they are needed.

10. Summarize what you have done so far. Your client has explored different ways in which people can be intrusive. She has identified her emotional response to intrusiveness and has prepared a set of things to say to people who are intrusive in different ways. Your client has also practiced these responses with you.

11. It's best to laminate those two cards. If you don't have access to a laminator, just use clear tape strips.

12. Assign homework: Ask your client to take the index cards home with her, carry them with her every day, and use them when appropriate. If the need to use them does not arise, ask your client to read both cards at the end of every day in order for the words to become familiar and comfortable.

13. Closing: Be sure to leave your client with words of encouragement, like:

    - *It's your story.*

    - *You don't have to tell it if you don't want to.*

    - *It's OK not to share when you don't want to.*

INTERVENTION 27

Being an Author

This intervention draws attention to the different ways in which your client can be the author of his own story. He can choose when and how to tell the story and decide which parts to tell and which to leave out. An emphasis on being an author can help your client overcome feelings of helplessness inherent in traumatic experiences. Your client did not choose his trauma, but he can write his own story.

Target skill: Owning the story. Creating the story.

What you will need: A roll of paper. If you do not have paper on a roll, simply tape together several sheets of paper to form a long strip. The strip should be at least four feet long in order to have as much space as is needed. Art materials such as markers, crayons, colored pencils, and writing tools.

1. Welcome your client. Ask questions like:

    - *How was the last week?*

    - *What were some choices you were able to make during the last week?*

    - *What were the situations in which you felt that you had little to no choice?*

    Listen reflectively. Give your client positive feedback for recognizing when he was able to make choices. If your client did make some choices, he has already taken a step out of helplessness. Help your client explore the situations in which he felt he had little to no choice. Keep in mind that there are some situations in which we all have fewer choices.

    - At work it's not a good idea to be late every day.

    - A student should do his or her homework.

    - Younger children can't really decide to walk out of class/not go to school.

    - Emphasize the choices that do exist, even in these situations.

    - I can be late for work every day (but may lose my job).

    - A student can decide not to do homework (but may have to stay after school to do it).

    - A young child can walk out of class (but will probably be brought into the office for consequences).

2. **Introduce today's task:** being the creative author of one's own story.

3. Review last week's homework. Ask questions like:

    - *Did you have an opportunity to use your response cards? If you did, how did it go? In what way did you feel you had a say? Was the person responsive?*

    - *If you did not have an opportunity to use the response cards, did you read them every day? How do you feel about the possibility of using them?*

    - *If your client would like some practice using them, now is a good time for a quick practice round.*

4. Work on today's task: Provide psychoeducation. You can say:

    There is always more than one way to tell a story. You can tell your story in the way that you want to tell it. It can have a lot of detail or be a general outline of what happened to you. You can write a book about your story or you can make a picture book. You can make your story into a song. No matter what, telling your story will help you contain your story. There is more to it than your traumatic experience. Let's take a look at what else there is.

5. Roll out the paper. Place the rolled-out paper in front of your client. Your client should be sitting facing the center of the roll like this:

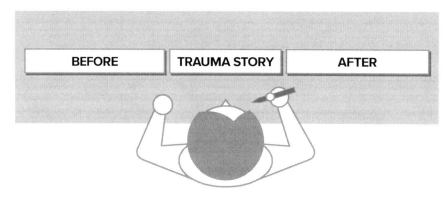

Figure 68

6. Explain that he is the author of his own story. The trauma story is very much front and center right now. It is right in front of him. Mark of a slice of the paper for the trauma story. You and your client have already reflected about the specific trauma story in the way your client wanted to. If it helps, place the trauma story in the center in the manner in which it was completed (artwork/story/book). Then ask your client to think, write, and draw about the time before the trauma. Ask questions like:

    - *Who was there?*
    - *Who was helpful?*
    - *What did you enjoy?*
    - *Who did you care about?*
    - *Where were you?*
    - *What places did you go to?*

    Ask your client to illustrate his life before the traumatic event. Share your client's excitement when it occurs. Pay attention to affect and relate to your client's experiences of connection and joy. If your client experienced developmental trauma, help him identify islands of safety he may have experienced.

7. Once your client has completed the "before the trauma" section, ask him to illustrate the "after the trauma" section. Part of his current experiences may go there. Also, ask your client to dream about his life in the future. Explain that, if necessary, more length can be added to the paper. This is a good way to illustrate that eventually there will be more of a distance between him and his traumatic story because there will have been so much more time and so many more experiences. Perhaps your client wants to picture himself as a nurse in the future. Or perhaps he wants to illustrate his dream vacation. Either way, he is becoming the author of his own story.

8. It may take more than one session to complete this intervention. This is OK. Once your client has completed the life story, help him reflect on it. You can ask/say:

   - *It looks like you have a lot of experiences ahead of you. Tell me more about . . .*

   - *It looks like you had experiences of connection/kindness/compassion in your past. Tell me more about those . . .*

   - *It looks like you have found a way to tell the story of your traumatic experience and put it in the context of your life. What does it feel like to look at the range of things that have happened, that are happening, and that you planned for and dreamed about?*

9. Summarize what you have done so far: Your client has explored ways in which his traumatic experience is just part—and not the only part—of the story of his life. Your client has reflected about the past and made plans for and dreamed about the future.

10. Assign homework: Send your client's "timeline" home with him. Ask him to post it somewhere prominent and then add to it as much as he wants. He can add by writing, drawing, or illustrating a specific event in any way. It's OK to add more paper. Ask him to bring the image to your next session.

11. Closing: Send your client home with words of encouragement, like:

   - *You did a great job bringing your story to life.*

   - *You did a great job thinking about the past and the future.*

   - *You created the story of your life, and there is so much more to come.*

INTERVENTION 28

Relating to Your Story

This intervention is designed to help your client explore her relationship with her story. At times the relationship can be rocky. The key is to help your client understand that she can choose, every day, how to relate to her story. She does not have to be "fused" with it (though some days it may feel like she is), and she can shape her story as it develops.

Target skill: Defusion. Flexibility. Self-compassion.

What you will need: Paper and writing/drawing tools. Markers. Index card.

1. Begin with empathy. Ask your client questions like:

   - *How was the last week?*

   - *In what way did you think about your story?*

   - *In what way did you just live your life?*

   Use reflective listening. Highlight all the ways in which your client was able to relate to her story without being swept away by it.

2. Introduce today's task: relating to one's own story in different ways.

3. Review last week's homework. Ask your client to take out her timeline. Take a look at it together.

   - What did your client add?

   - Are there other things your client would like to add now?

   Use reflective listening and highlight all the ways in which your client is expanding and authoring her story.

4. Work on today's task: Provide psychoeducation. You can say:

   Traumatic experiences tend to take away our choices. They tell us that there are only a few things we can do: Run, fight, or hide. But in reality, once the traumatic experience is over, we can relate to it in many different ways. This intervention is designed to help you explore the different ways in which you may want to and can relate to your story.

5. Begin by asking your client about different ways she may relate to different people. You can ask:

   - *How do you relate to people who are kind to you?*

   - *How do you relate to people who love you the most?*

   - *How do you relate to people who bug you?*

   - *How about people who are annoying?*

   - *And people who ask too much of you?*

   - *What about people you want to see?*

   - *What about people you don't want to see?*

- *How about people you need a break from?*

6. While your client is giving you the answers, use a marker to write them on a large piece of paper. Once your list is complete, ask your client to explore the idea that she can relate to her story in different ways. Here are some possibilities if your client needs help with this:

    - She can be kind to her story.

    - She can love her story (which is different than loving what happened to her).

    - She can "shoo" the story away when needed.

    - She can be annoyed by it.

    - She can be tired of it.

    - She can invite it in.

    - She can decline to invite it in.

    - She can leave it be for a minute or a day.

    - She can embrace it with compassion.

    Help your client be specific about the different ways in which she can relate to her story. Normalize the experience that relating to her story can change over time, sometimes in the course of a day. The important part of this intervention is for your client to learn that she has a relationship with her story, and she can change it in the ways that "fit" her context on any given day. She is in control.

7. Should the story feel threatening at any time, ask your client to resort to compassion with both herself and the story. Your client can say: "I can be patient with myself and the story. I can be kind to myself and the story. I can have compassion for myself and the story." Write these sentences on an index card for your client to take home.

8. Review what you have done so far: You have explored the different ways in which your client can relate to those around her and her story. You have explored the idea that your client's relationships with her story can change over time and that she can add compassion to her relationship with herself and her story any time this is needed.

9. Assign homework: Send home the following index card. You may want to laminate it.

I can be patient
with myself and my story.

I can be kind
to myself and my story.

I can have compassion
for myself and my story.

Figure 69

Ask your client to observe, at least once every day, the way she relates to her story and make a note of this on the back of the index card. Ask your client to bring the card back to your next meeting.

10. Closing: Send your client home with words of encouragement, like:

- *It's OK to have a different relationship with your story on different days.*

- *When in doubt, go back to compassion with yourself and your story.*

Interventions for Building a Life

If you have experienced trauma or long periods of toxic stress, the past is always calling you. Because those experiences were emotionally intense and distressing, there is a "pull" to go back to them. Part of recovering from traumatic experiences is building a life in the present and the future, to truly be here now and also look ahead to what is to come.

To some trauma survivors, this can feel like a betrayal of the past. If this is the case, the task is to honor the past *and* the present and future, to understand that these things are not mutually exclusive. Building a life is never about forgetting the past.

The following interventions are designed to help your client reflect on this process of building a life while integrating and honoring the past.

INTERVENTION 29

Both Ways: There and Then and Here and Now

This intervention is designed to help your client explore and understand the fundamental human task of remembering and honoring the past while fully living in the present. This task is complicated for trauma survivors and those who have experienced long periods of toxic stress. These experiences have shaped who they are, and if you think of them in this way, it is neither necessary nor desirable to forget about them.

Target skill: Mindful presence. Honoring the past. Moving freely between memory and presence.

What you will need: Image of a timeline (see below). Writing and drawing tools.

1. Begin with empathy. Welcome your client and ask questions like:

   - *How was the last week?*

   - *Is there anything new to reflect on?*

   - *How does your client feel today about being the author of his story as it evolves?*

   Listen reflectively and highlight your client's efforts to take charge of his story.

2. **Introduce today's task:** mindful presence with the past and the here and now.

3. Review last week's homework. Ask your client to take out last week's index card. Take a look at the back together.

   - In what way has your client related to his story this week?

   - When did he feel happy about his story and how it evolved?

   - When did he want to "shoo" it away?

   - In what way was your client able to be nonjudgmental about himself and his story?

   Remember: The key is to help your client understand that he can relate to his story. It is not his trauma that dictates the relationship. He can make choices.

4. Work on today's task: being there and then (remembering the past without being overcome by it) and here and now, and moving freely between them. Provide psychoeducation. You can say this:

   What we do today is designed to help you explore and understand the fundamental human task of remembering and honoring the past while fully living in the present. This task can be complicated for trauma survivors and those who have experienced long periods of toxic stress. These experiences may have shaped who you are, and if you think of them in this way it is neither necessary nor desirable to forget about them. But it is important to also live in the present.

5.   Provide your client with a timeline for his life. Briefly review her story with him, including the past and the present.

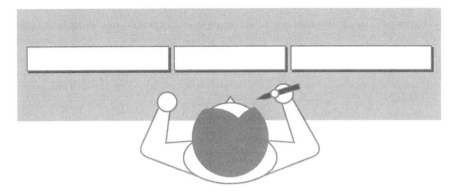

Figure 70

Help him explore the current ways in which he manages the relationship between the past and the present. You can ask:

- *In what way do you go back and forth between thinking about the past and the present?*

- *In what way is this comfortable? What makes you uncomfortable about it?*

- *How important is the separation between the past and the present for you?*

- *How do you pay attention to the past? How about the present?*

Listen reflectively and highlight your client's efforts to move between the past and the present as he would like to, even if with difficulty.

6.   Move into reflection. Create a column for the past and the present. If it helps, you may want to line it up under the timeline. Ask your client to identify ways in which he honors and recognizes the past and ways in which he is fully present in the here and now. Then, add an additional box for new ideas.

I honor the past by:	I am fully present in the here and now by:
◄ I am able to move back and forth as I wish and need to! ►	
New ideas for honoring the past:	New ideas for being fully present in the here and now:

Figure 71

Continue to help your client recognize that he can shape her relationship with his story. The more he actively and consciously does so, the less he may be bothered by unwanted intrusions from the past. To help your client with this, you can ask:

- *What part of your story do you want to be fully present with now?*

- *Who do you want to share this part of the story with?*

If your client struggles with identifying ideas for honoring the past and being fully present now, you can provide a list of ideas like:

- Light a candle to honor the past.

- Create and keep a memory book.

- Create a collage about the past.

- Reconnect with important people from the past.

- Read about overcoming trauma and stress.

- Give a speech about overcoming trauma.

- Become active in child abuse or domestic violence prevention.

- Engage to help others out of extreme poverty.

- Become a mentor.
- Do yoga or tai chi.
- Pray or meditate.
- Experience joy.
- Enter into safe and supportive relationships.
- Cook.
- Eat mindfully.
- Sing.
- Fix up an old car or bike.
- Help your neighbor.
- Garden.
- Spend time with your pet.
- Walk.
- Paint, color, or draw.

You can see that this list could be endless, and you can add suggestions better suited to your client. Keep in mind that sometimes your client may have to "try on" a way of being present in order to know if it will "fit."

7. Review what you have done so far: Your client has briefly explored his story and how he relates to it. He has then explored ways in which he can honor the past and live fully in the present.

8. Assign homework: Send the list of activities home with your client. Ask him to engage in at least one activity on the list every day, then record that activity. Ask your client to bring the checked list back to your next meeting.

9. Closing: Leave your client with words of encouragement, like:

   - Being fully present is possible.
   - Honoring the past without being overcome by it is possible.
   - There is no need for perfection. Just living will do.

INTERVENTION 30

Daring to Look Ahead

Those who have survived trauma and toxic stress can struggle to believe that there might be any kind of future for them. This makes sense and can also serve an adaptive function. All energy is spent on survival. When the focus in on survival, there is not energy left to think about the future. All that matters is the ability to fight, run, or hide. Additionally, it may be easier to simply give up on the future, to avoid disappointment.

Looking ahead is a shift. It requires the ability (acquired by practice) to think about the future and plan for it. Doing so is an incredibly courageous step for trauma survivors. It means that they are daring to hope.

Target skill: Planning. Dreaming. Living beyond pain.

What you will need: Poster board. Markers. Drawing tools.

1. Begin with empathy. Welcome your client and ask questions like:

   - *How was your week?*

   - *In what way have you thought about the future?*

   - *In what way have you had hope?*

   Listen reflectively and highlight any effort by your client to think ahead. Any of these efforts, no matter how small, signal the ability to defuse from a life story that is held hostage by trauma and toxic stress.

2. **Introduce today's task:** daring to look ahead.

3. Review last week's homework. Ask your client to take out the activity list and review it together. Which activities did your client use to honor the past? Which activities did your client use to be fully present in the here and now? Then ask:

   - *What worked?*

   - *What did not work?*

   - *How did you feel after each activity?*

   - *What was it like to go back and forth between the present and the past?*

   - *In what way are you becoming more comfortable doing so?*

   - *When and how is this still difficult?*

   Encourage your client to continue to identify new ways of honoring the past and living in the present that will work for her, and to take time for this every day.

4. Work on today's task: Provide psychoeducation. You can say:

   Thinking about and planning for the future can be difficult for survivors of trauma and toxic stress. When the focus has been on survival for a long time, making plans can seem frivolous or even downright silly. Why would one make plans when one does not expect to survive or have any kind of say in their life? Yet there is another way of living. When the danger has passed, you can emerge out of your survival state and begin to think about the future, the kind of future that you want to build. This can be difficult at first, but it's an important part of reclaiming one's life. Looking ahead is an expression of hope. You have survived. It is OK now to hope and dream.

5. Work on today's task: Provide your client with a large poster board. Help her explore the kinds of things that have been in the back of her mind waiting to be thought about. Here are some questions to get your client started:

- *Where do you want to live?*
- *How do you want to live?*
- *Who do you really want with you?*
- *What do you need in your place to be comfortable?*
- *What will you do for a living?*
- *What will you do for relaxation?*
- *What adventures would you like to have?*
- *Where do you want to go, near and far?*
- *What hobby do you want to pick up?*
- *What would you like to learn?*
- *What friendships would you like to build?*
- *Are you interested in a spiritual community?*
- *Are there any pets you would like?*

Ask your client to use the poster board to illustrate her dreams/plans for the future. Explain that this activity is not about neatness. Your client can draw, write, paint, doodle, glue, or whatever else works. Plans don't have to be detailed or neat. They can be presented in the form of ideas.

If your client is looking for a way to begin, here is an idea:

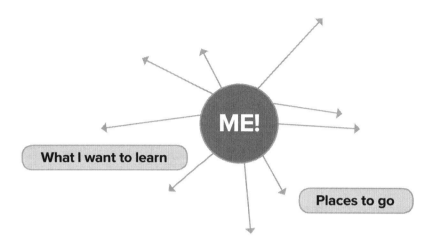

Figure 72

Your client can add as many arrows as needed.

6. When your client has completed her work, help her reflect. Provide positive feedback for stepping out of survival mode and daring to dream. Ask questions like:

    - *What is most important to you right now?*

    - *Where do you want to start?*

    - *Which is the most practical hope?*

    - *Which one is easiest to begin with?*

    If your client falls back into trauma/survival mode and feels overwhelmed, help her defuse from this by saying:

    - *It looks like you are feeling overwhelmed.*

    - *Just breathe with me right now.*

    - *None of this has to happen today or very fast.*

    - *You choose what becomes real, and you set the pace.*

    - *It's good to have help when making plans and dreaming. You are not alone! Let's think about who will be by your side. Part of moving beyond a trauma-focused life is building connections of hope.*

7. Once your client has reflected on her dreams and plans for the future, help her step back and look at the picture she has created. The image in itself may be beautiful or interesting. It could be messy or organized. Help your client explore the idea that she can create, here and now, a beautiful or interesting work of art. Ask her to enjoy the image and give her positive feedback about it.

8. Summarize what you have done so far: Your client has explored the impact trauma and stress can have on future planning. Your client has created an

image containing dreams and future plans. She has also learned to appreciate the image.

9. Assign homework: Give the poster board to your client to take home. Ask her to add to it over the course of the next week. She can write, draw, or paint on it. She can glue things on it. She can add to its size by taping pages. She can place inspirational items or photos next to it. Then ask her to bring the image to your next meeting.

10. Closing: Leave your client with words of encouragement, like:

   - *You can dream now.*
   - *It's OK to dream big and small.*
   - *Bringing dreams to life can be learned.*
   - *It's OK to take time with all of this! There is no pressure.*

INTERVENTION 31

With Care

The following intervention is designed to infuse mindfulness and compassion into all future planning. Mindfulness and self-compassion will serve as a counterbalance to the tendency to do all or fix all in a hurry.

Target skill: Infusing mindfulness and self-compassion into planning.

What you will need: Simple item(s) to hold and focus on, such as a smooth stone, a flower, a marble, a stuffed animal, or a doll.

1. Welcome your client and begin with empathy. Ask questions like:

   - *How was the last week?*

   - *What does it feel like to focus more on the future and less on the past?*

   - *What do you need to feel supported in this focus on the future?*

   Listen reflectively and highlight any efforts by your client to plan for and focus on the future.

2. **Introduce today's task:** planning and dreaming for the future with care and self-compassion.

3. Review last week's homework. Ask your client to take out his poster board, and look at it together. What did your client add and why? Did he cross out anything? Are there any items he would have liked to add but were too big or too precious to attach? What did it feel like to look at the picture?

4. Explain that the image is a work in progress, as planning for the future should be. It's perfect when it is imperfect! Pay attention to affect, and highlight any excitement you see in your client about planning for the future.

5. Work on today's task: Provide psychoeducation. You can say: Trauma puts us in survival mode. When we are in survival mode we can't really take time to be kind and compassionate to ourselves and do things with care. Now that the danger has passed, it's OK to be more planful, kind, and compassionate with yourself. The mindful approach to doing this will be helpful for you for years to come.

6. Ask your client to begin by engaging in the following exercise: Give him a small item to hold (such as a smooth rock, marble, etc.). Ask him to "just hold it." After a few seconds have passed, ask him to hold it "with care." Watch what happens.

7. Ask your client questions like:

   - *Did anything change when I asked you to hold the item with care?*

   - *Did you shift? Do something different with your hands?*

   - *Did you wonder, what does it mean to "hold with care"?*

   - *Did you feel differently toward the item?*

8. Ask your client to name one of his dreams for the future, then ask him to add the words "with care" to that dream/hope. Here is an example:

Perhaps your client wants to be in a relationship. Ask him to say: "I want to be in a relationship—with care." Then ask him to reflect:

- *What happens when you add "with care" to your dream/plan/hope?*

Repeat the exercise with several of your client's dreams/plans/hopes.

9. Introduce the idea of self-compassion. You can define self-compassion as the willingness to be kind and caring toward oneself. Connect the idea of adding the words "with care" to dreams/hopes/plans with the idea of self-compassion. You can say: "When you are adding the words 'with care' to your plans, you are adding a dose of self-compassion. Trauma teaches you to be harsh with yourself so you can survive. Now that the danger is over, it's OK to be compassionate toward yourself."

10. What if your client hates the idea of self-compassion? Introduce the idea of being kinder to oneself and walking toward self-compassion. Assure your client that self- compassion is not "sappy." Think of a carpenter. It's better to hammer the nail into the wall "with care" to avoid getting hurt. There is nothing sappy about that.

11. Review what you have done so far: Your client has explored how trauma and stress can impact our capacity to be kind to ourselves. Your client has engaged in an experiment to explore how doing something with care differs from just doing it. You have then explored the idea of approaching dreams and plans for the future with care and have linked this idea with the concept of self-compassion.

12. Assign homework. Give your client the following index card:

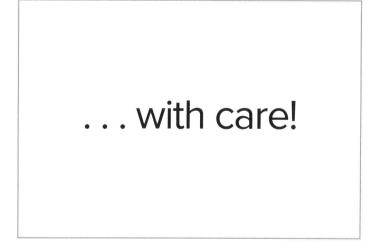

Figure 73

Ask him to carry the card with him and use it every time he feels unkind, harsh, or judgmental toward himself. Ask him to use the card to remind himself to be self-compassionate and to bring the card back to your next meeting. Here is an example:

Your client is in a hurry. He is already late for something. Instead of engaging in self-deprecating talk, he could say: "I will get ready with care. I will travel with care."

13. Closing: Send your client home with words of care, like:

- *Being kind to yourself makes a difference.*

- *Being unkind to yourself generally makes things worse.*

- *You deserve kindness by others and yourself.*

INTERVENTION 32

Living as if It Already Were True

For some people it can be difficult to dream about and plan for the future. Those who have survived traumatic and stressful experiences are often stuck in survival mode, where the only thing that counts is the ability to make it through another day. Dreaming and planning take time and energy, and "the future" may seem too distant to think about today. The following intervention asks your client to bring the future into the present.

Target skill: Planning. Operationalizing (bringing to life and making it real).

What you will need: Schedule for a day. Writing and drawing tools. Index cards.

1. Begin with empathy. Welcome your client and ask questions like:

    - *How was the last week?*

    - *Who was kind to you?*

    - *Who were you kind to?*

    Overall, how able was she to live well with her symptoms of trauma? You can use the following scale to help her answer this question:

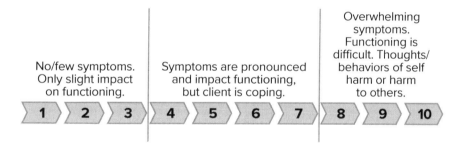

Figure 74

    When your client answers this question, explore treatment progress overall. Begin to explore termination of services. You may want to help your client explore the idea that recovery can not only be defined by diminished symptoms but should be defined, even more so, by the ability to live well in spite of symptoms.

2. **Introduce today's task:** living as if your plans and dreams were already becoming real.

3. Review last week's homework. Ask your client to take out her Kindness Card and to explore with you opportunities for self-compassion that occurred in the course of the last week. You can ask:

    - *When did you have opportunity to use this card?*

    - *What happened that made you take out the card?*

    - *How did you feel about using the card?*

- *In what way were you kinder to yourself after using the card?*

If your client did not use the card, ask why. If your client was able to be kind to herself without using the card, this is, of course, OK. Still, ask for examples of self-compassion, then give your client positive feedback about being kind to herself.

4. Work on today's task: Provide psychoeducation. You can say:

    Think about your future as beginning right now. The future is not some abstract thing that happens in a faraway place and time. Think about it this way: The future could be one minute from now when your child comes running toward you and you are being kind to yourself and your child. The future could be tomorrow, when you finally go to that yoga class you have been thinking about for a year. Or the future could be next week, when you enroll in that job-training program you are really interested in. So when you think about that yoga class, you are already "futuring," engaging in a positive interaction with your future.

5. Ask your client to recall two components of her dreams and plans for the future. Then help her develop a way to engage with her future today. You can use the following image to do so:

Figure 75

Ask your client in what way she can "future" today by doing at least three things that approximate what she wants her future to be like. Perhaps your client wants to be in a loving relationship. In what way can she be the source of love and compassion today?

Help your client understand that there is a feedback loop. Dreams and future plans impact how she lives today, and how she lives today impacts her dreams and plans for the future. This positive feedback loop will help your client build her future.

A negative feedback loop would sound like this: Your client has big dreams and plans for the future. They are so big—and overwhelming—that she feels there is nothing to do but throw her hands in the air and despair about how impossible everything is. The key to creating a positive feedback loop is to do things that are possible today.

Your client can complete the image above in any way she wants. She can write or draw. Children or creative adults may need more space. Just use single sheets of paper to outline each activity today that relates to the future.

If you are working with a child, you may want to describe the activity by saying something like: *Think about right now. What part of your dream or plan can you already practice right now?*

6. Review what you have done so far: Your client has explored dreams and plans for the future. You have explored how the future relates to the present and identified ways in which your client can connect with her future right now by doing things that prepare her for the kind of future she wants.

7. Assign homework: Ask your client to pick one of the actions she outlined above. Take an index card and write this action on it. Ask your client to take the card home and engage in that action at least once every day, then place a check mark on the day the action was performed. Ask your client to bring the card back to your next meeting.

Every day I will _____ to prepare for the future I want.
Monday:
Tuesday:
Wednesday:
Thursday:
Friday:
Saturday:
Sunday:

Figure 76

8.   Closing: Leave your client with words of encouragement, like:

- *You can work toward the future you want today.*

- *You can bring your future to life.*

- *Every little action counts.*

INTERVENTION 33

On the Road

When it is time to discontinue services, it might be helpful to use a metaphor to describe what is ahead. While the discontinuing treatment is the end of something, it really is the beginning of something else: your client's continued journey toward the life he wants, which is unfolding every day. The following intervention is designed to help your client recognize the progress he has made and will continue to make on his journey.

Target skill: Moving forward and looking back.

What you will need: Cardboard or other type of box. Materials for decorating the box (arts and craft materials, including scissors and glue). Drawing and writing tools. Special item.

1. Begin with empathy. Welcome your client and ask questions like:

    - *What does it feel like to be almost done?*

    - *What are your hopes and fears?*

    - *What are you proud of?*

    Listen reflectively and highlight your client's abilities in managing symptoms. You might say things like:

    - *When you first started coming here, you were so afraid of everything. Now you know what to do when you feel overwhelmed.*

    - *When I first met you, it was difficult for you to trust anyone. Now you have a group of friends you trust, and this groups supports you.*

    - *When we first met, you thought nothing and nobody could possibly help you. Now you know what to do when you feel sad, angry, overwhelmed, and anxious.*

2. **Introduce today's task:** thinking of oneself on the road to living mindfully and wholeheartedly.

3. Review last week's homework. Ask your client to take out his action card. Take a look at it together. Ask:

    - *Which action did you engage in?*

    - *How did this action make a difference?*

    - *In what way did this action prepare you for the future or bring about part of the future?*

    Listen reflectively and highlight your client's ability to defuse from the past, be present in the moment, and look toward the future.

4. Work on today's task: Provide psychoeducation. You can say this:

    Some people think that in order to be well, they should be symptom-free. The truth is that symptoms can get better, and some symptoms can even go away. Being able to fully live in spite of remaining symptoms, however,

*is the true mark of a survivor. Life will leave its marks. Some cannot be
erased. But life can continue. You can build the life you want, and you have
done a lot of this in treatment. Today is about celebrating the road traveled,
the road to come, and preparing for what is ahead.*

5. Explain that you will be creating a toolbox for your client to take home.
    Provide the box and art materials. Ask him to decorate the box in any way
    he wants. You may want to provide ribbons and beads, pictures of tools and
    cartoon characters, or images of superheroes. Anything that you know is
    precious to your client will work. While your client is decorating the box,
    explain that the box will go home with him and be filled with all the ideas,
    goals, coping skills, and memories that will help him move forward.

6. Once the box is decorated, help your client identify all of the things that will
    help him on his travels (tools for ongoing recovery/tools for life). It can be
    helpful to create the following categories:

    - Values

    - Goals

    - Coping skills

    - Memories

    - Companions

    Of course, you can add any category you want.

7. Give your client index cards and ask him to "fill the categories." Anything
    that you have explored, built, or created to help your client in his recovery
    should be written or drawn on those index cards. As your client is naming
    these things, help him review them and their meaning in his recovery.

8. Put all of the cards in the toolbox. Then provide your client with an item that
    is meaningful to him, such as a smooth stone. This is a "transitional object"
    that he can carry with him to symbolize your work together and remind him
    of what he has learned. It can be helpful to have a box of those kinds of items
    to choose from. If your client chooses, this is once again an opportunity to
    explore how this item is meaningful to him and his recovery. Items do not
    have to be expensive, just meaningful.

9. Review what you have done together: You have created a toolbox for your
    client to take home. The toolbox contains all the things that have helped
    him in his recovery and will continue to help him in the future. You have
    included a special item in the toolbox that will serve as a reminder of your
    time together.

10. Provide information about returning to therapy as needed. You can say this:
    You are ready to move on. You have learned so much. You know your coping
    skills. You have friends who surround you when this is needed. It is possible
    that at some point in the future you may need some more help with your
    recovery. This is OK. As you already know, there is no shame in needing
    help. For now, though, you are good to go!

11. Be sure to provide contact information (such as the number for Central Intake).

12. Closing: Send your client home with the toolbox and thank him for trusting you to help him in his recovery. It's good to say something like:

> *It was a great honor to help you. You have done so much work. You can be proud of the work you have done and the life you live!*

Appendix: Selected Figures

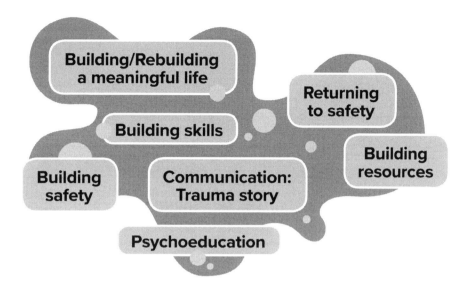

Figure 1

Course/Length of Treatment

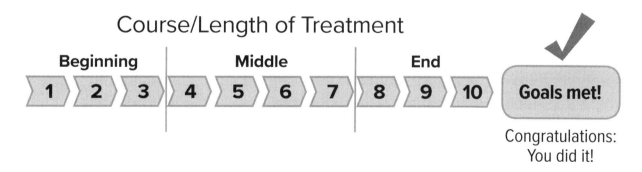

Figure 14

CBT Session Structure
Check-In
Identify Today's Task
Homework Review
Work on Today's Task
Summarize the Work
Identify New Homework
Closing

Figure 15

	Mon	Tue	Wed	Thu	Fri	Sat	Sun
Hours in bed							
Hours of TV							

Figure 16

	Mon	Tue	Wed	Thu	Fri	Sat	Sun
Contacted friend/family member X							

Figure 17

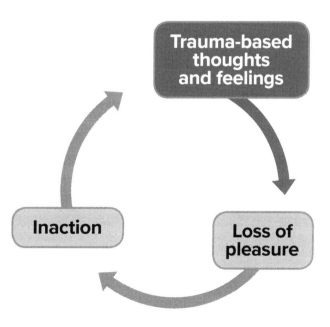

Figure 18

186

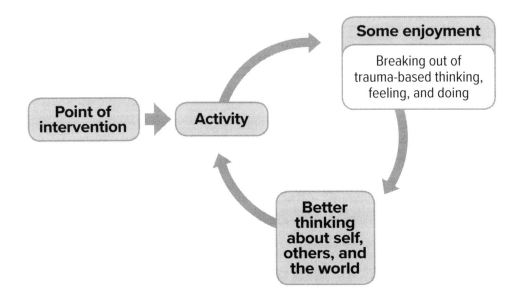

Figure 19

	Morning	Afternoon	Evening
Mon			
Tue			
Wed			
Thu			
Fri			
Sat			
Sun			

Figure 20

Automatic Thought	Evidence for AT	Evidence against AT

Figure 22

Figure 25

Daily Safe Space:
Monday:
Tuesday:
Wednesday:
Thursday:
Friday:
Saturday:
Sunday:

Figure 26

Spending time with my person/pet:
Monday:
Tuesday:
Wednesday:
Thursday:
Friday:
Saturday:
Sunday:

Figure 28

Ask your client to inhale, slowly and naturally, through her nose.

Ask your client to exhale, slowly and naturally, through her mouth.

Figure 29

Feelings are **manageable**.   Feelings are **difficult** but manageable.   Feelings seem **out of control**.

Figure 30

Volunteer activity:	Date and time to complete:
Call three organizations for information	
Schedule appointments to visit	
Visit organization 1	
Visit organization 2	
Visit organization 3	
Make a choice	
Schedule weekly appointments for volunteering	

Figure 31

	Mindful Presence Practice 1	Mindful Presence Practice 2
Mon		
Tue		
Wed		
Thu		
Fri		
Sat		
Sun		

Figure 32

Joyful Presence through Motion:
Monday:
Tuesday:
Wednesday:
Thursday:
Friday:
Saturday:
Sunday:

Figure 33

Figure 34

What my body needs:	What I can do about this:	When can I do this:

Figure 36

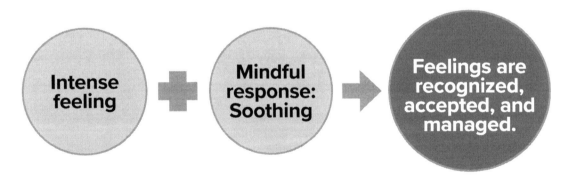

Figure 38

Feelings are **manageable**.	Feelings are **difficult** but manageable.	Feelings seem **out of control**.
1 2 3	4 5 6 7	8 9 10

Figure 39

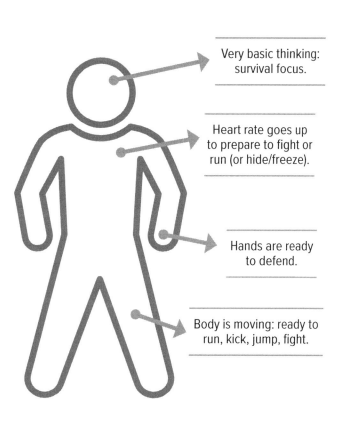

Very basic thinking: survival focus.

Heart rate goes up to prepare to fight or run (or hide/freeze).

Hands are ready to defend.

Body is moving: ready to run, kick, jump, fight.

Figure 40

What my brain needs:	What I can do about this:	When can I do this:

Figure 41

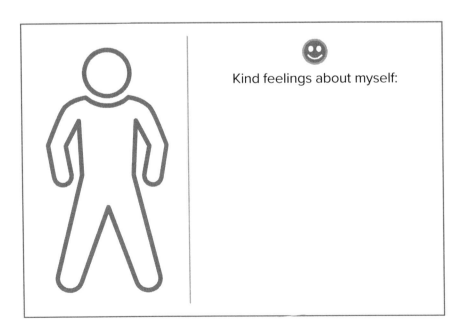

Figure 43

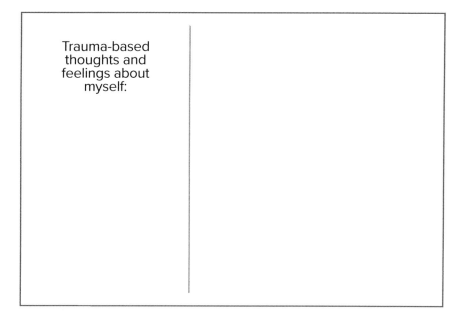

Trauma-based thoughts and feelings about myself:

Figure 44

I will be kind to myself by . . .
Monday:
Tuesday:
Wednesday:
Thursday:
Friday:
Saturday:
Sunday:

Figure 45

196

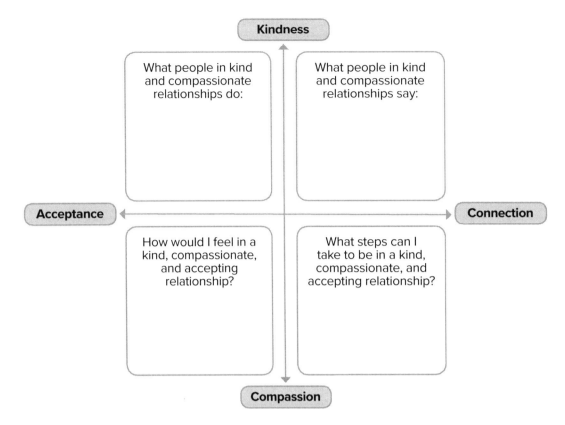

Figure 46

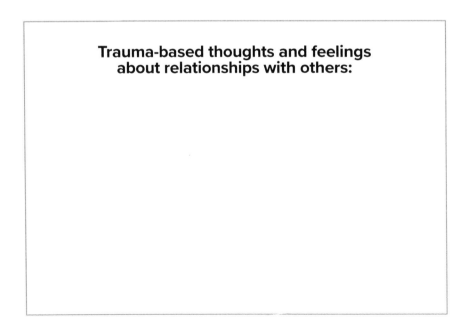

Figure 47

	Person:	Person:
What in this relationship is kind, compassionate and accepting:		
What in this relationship is trauma-based?		

Figure 48

Be Well Chart		
To eat well, I will:	To sleep well, I will:	To be connected, I will:

Figure 49

I will practice being well by . . .
Monday:
Tuesday:
Wednesday:
Thursday:
Friday:
Saturday:
Sunday:

Figure 50

Overall Goal: Obtain Meaningful Employment			
Step 1: Clarification of goal			
Date to begin:			
Date to finish:			
Step 2: Action Plan			
Date to begin:			
Date to finish:			
Step 3: Moving ahead			
Date to begin:			
Date to finish			

Figure 51

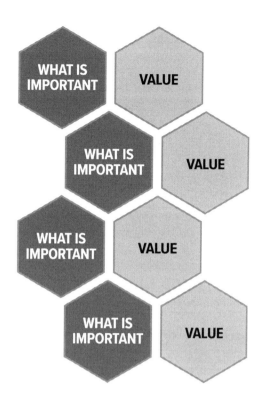

Figure 52

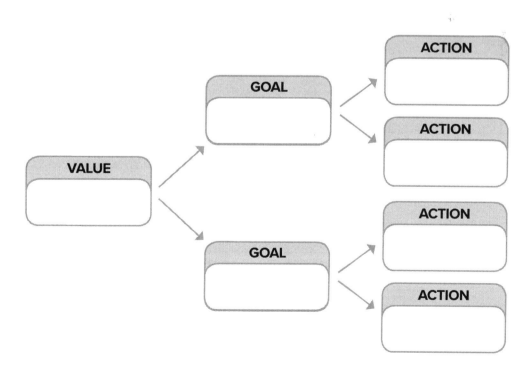

Figure 54

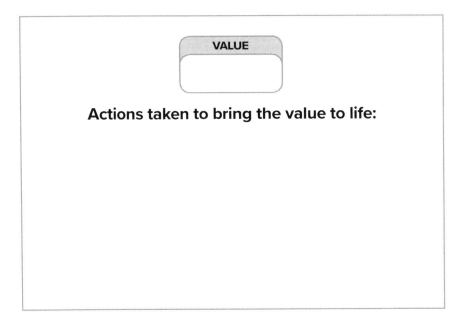

Figure 55

Figure 56

Figure 57

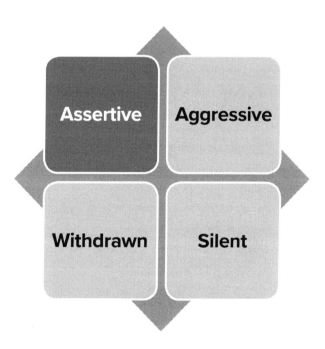

Figure 58

Feeling: Intensity of feeling on
a scale from 1–10 (10 being the highest):

Related to **current** situation in the following way:

Related to **past** situation in the following way:

Examining the situation—stepping back:

Turning the volume of the feeling
up/down—how to ideas:

Figure 59

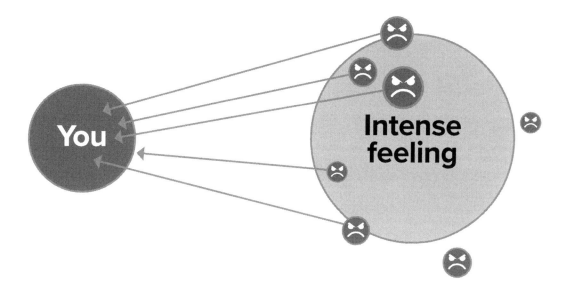

Figure 60

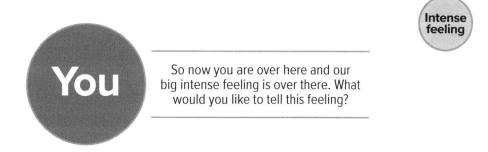

Figure 61

**Steps to take to separate
from a big, intense feeling:**

1. Greet the feeling.

2. Name the feeling.

3. Welcome the feeling.

4. Do the following to gain distance from the feeling:

- _____

- _____

- _____

- _____

Figure 62

MINDFUL TRUST

- Discussed with family/friends
- History together
- Took time to trust
- Thought things through
- Person of character

IMPULSIVE TRUST

- Did not discuss
- Little history together
- Quick decision
- Emotional decision
- Controlling/angry person

Figure 63

Opening and closing the story:
Monday:
Tuesday:
Wednesday:
Thursday:
Friday:
Saturday:
Sunday:

Figure 65

What to say to someone who is trying to be helpful but really does not understand:

1. I understand you are trying to help,

2. but _____ ,

3. and _____ ,

4. so, _____ .

Figure 66

**What to say to someone who
is intrusive and uncaring:**

5. This is not your business.

6. I am asking you to _____ .

7. I need you to quit _____ .

8. Otherwise I may have to _____ .

Figure 67

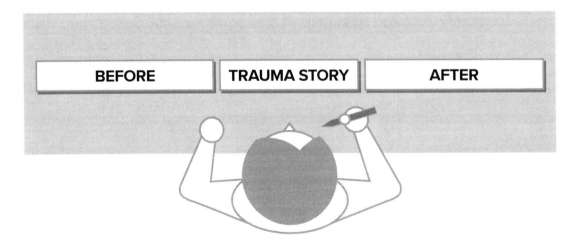

Figure 68

I can be patient
with myself and my story.

I can be kind
to myself and my story.

I can have compassion
for myself and my story.

Figure 69

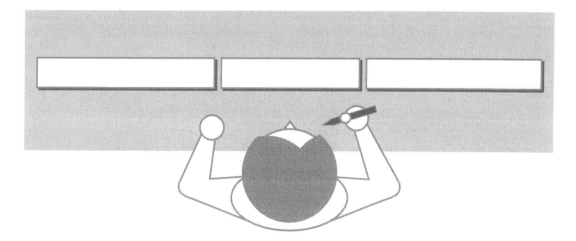

Figure 70

I honor the past by:	I am fully present in the here and now by:
◄ I am able to move back and forth as I wish and need to! ►	
New ideas for honoring the past:	New ideas for being fully present in the here and now:

Figure 71

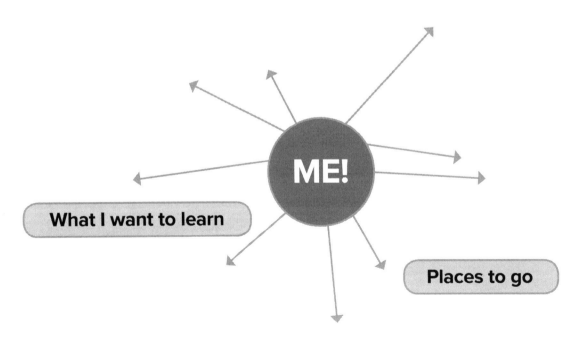

Figure 72

... with care!

Figure 73

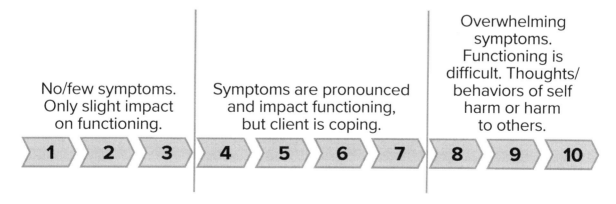

Figure 74

210

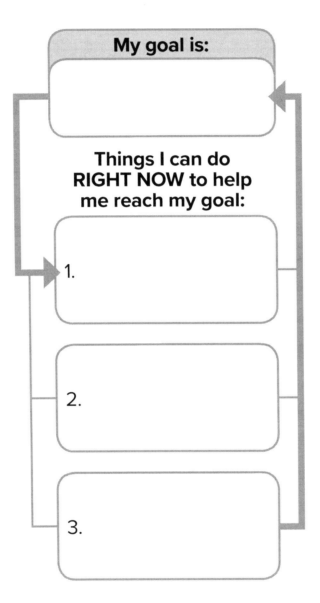

Figure 75

Every day I will _____ to prepare for the future I want.
Monday:
Tuesday:
Wednesday:
Thursday:
Friday:
Saturday:
Sunday:

Figure 76

References

ACES too high (2017). ACES too high. Retrieved from https://acestoohigh.com/aces-101/

American Psychiatric Association. (2013). *Diagnostic and statistical manual of mental disorders* (5th ed.). Arlington, VA: American Psychiatric Publishing.

American Psychological Association. (2017). *Clinical practice guideline for the treatment of PTSD.* Washington, D.C.: APA. Retrieved from http://www.apa.org/ptsd-guideline/ptsd.pdf

Australian Childhood Foundation. (2011). Discussion paper 18: Polyvagal theory and its implications for traumatised students. Australia: SMART.

Beck, A. T., Rush, A. J., Shaw, B. F., & Emery, G. (1979). *Cognitive therapy of depression.* New York, NY: Guilford Press.

Berenz, E. C., & Coffey, S. F. (2012). Treatment of co-occurring posttraumatic stress disorder and substance use disorders. *Current Psychiatry Reports, 14*(5), 469-477. doi:10.1007/s11920-012-0300-0

California Evidence-Based Clearing House for Child Welfare. (2015, December). Retrieved from http://www.cebc4cw.org/program/child-parent-psychotherapy/detailed

Child Welfare Information Gateway. (2015). Understanding the effects of maltreatment on brain development. Washington, DC: U.S. Department of Health and Human Services, Children's Bureau. Retrieved from https://www.childwelfare.gov/pubPDFs/brain_development.pdf

Cohen, J. A., Mannarino, A. P., & Deblinger, E. (2016). *Trauma-focused CBT for children and adolescents: Treatment applications.* New York, NY: Guilford Press.

Cohen, J. (2016). Trauma-focused cognitive behavioral therapy (TF-CBT). Retrieved from https://www.nrepp.samhsa.gov/ProgramProfile.aspx?id=96

Courtois, C. A., & Ford, J. D. (2014). *Treating complex traumatic stress disorders in children and adolescents: Scientific foundations and therapeutic models.* New York, NY: Guilford Press.

Dobson, D., & Dobson, K. (2017). *Evidence-based practice of cognitive behavioral therapy.* New York, NY: Guilford Press.

Fefergrad, M., & Maunder, R. (2013). *Psychotherapy essentials to go: Cognitive behavioral therapy for depression.* New York, NY: Norton & Company.

Fisher, J. E., & O'Donohue, W. (2006). The *practitioner's guide to evidence-based psychotherapy.* New York, NY: Springer.

Ford, J. D., & Cloitre, M. (2009). Best practices in psychotherapy for children and adolescents. In *Treating complex traumatic stress disorders: Scientific foundations and therapeutic models* (pp. 59-81). New York, NY: Guilford Press.

Ford, J. D., & Courtois, C. A. (2016). Treating complex traumatic stress disorders in children and adolescents: Scientific foundations and therapeutic models. New York, NY: Guilford Press.

Harris, R. (2009). *ACT made simple: An easy-to-read primer on acceptance and commitment therapy*. Oakland, CA: New Harbinger Publications.

International Society for Traumatic Stress Studies. (n.d.). Retrieved from https://www.istss.org/

Jong, P. D., & Berg, I. K. (2013). *Interviewing for solutions*. South Melbourne, Australia: Brooks/Cole, Cengage Learning.

Najavits, L. M. (2003). *Seeking safety: A treatment manual for PTSD and substance abuse*. New York, NY: Guilford Press.

Narváez, D. (2014). *Neurobiology and the development of human morality: Evolution, culture, and wisdom*. New York, NY: W. W. Norton.

Neff, K. (2013). *Self compassion*. London: Hodder & Stoughton.

Persons, J. B, Davidson, J., & Tompkins, M. A. (2001). *Essential components of cognitive behavioral therapy for depression*. Washington, DC: American Psychological Association.

Porges, S. W. (2011). *The polyvagal theory: Neurophysiological foundations of emotions, attachment, communication, and self-regulation*. New York, NY: W. W. Norton.

SAMHSA's National Registry of Evidence-based Programs and Practices. (2017). Screening and treatment for posttraumatic stress disorder. Evidence summary. Rockville, MD: Substance Abuse and Mental Health Services Administration. Retrieved from https://nrepp-learning.samhsa.gov/sites/default/files/documents/Topics_Behavioral_Health/pdf_07_2017/Screening%20and%20Treatment%20for%20Posttraumatic%20Stress%20Disorder_7.2017.pdf

Schore, A. N. (2016). *Affect regulation and the origin of the self: The neurobiology of emotional development*. New York, NY: Psychology Press.

Schore, J. R., & Schore, A. N. (2007). Modern attachment theory: The central role of affect regulation in development and treatment. *Clinical Social Work Journal, 36*(1), 9-20. doi:10.1007/s10615-007-0111-7

Scott Heller, S. & Gilkerson, L. (2009). *A practical guide to reflective supervision*. Washington, D.C.: Zero to Three.

Seeking Safety for PTSD with Substance Use Disorder. (2016). Retrieved from https://www.div12.org/treatment/seeking-safety-for-ptsd-with-substance-use-disorder/

Stamm, B. H., (2009). *Professional quality of life: Compassion satisfaction and fatigue version 5*: ProQOL. Retrieved from http://www.proqol.org/uploads/ProQOL_5_English_Self-Score_3-2012.pdf

Treatment Innovations. (2016). Retrieved from https://www.treatment-innovations.org/

Tolin, D. F. (2016). *Doing CBT: A comprehensive guide to working with behaviors, thoughts, and emotions*. New York, NY: Guilford Press.

Van Der Kolk, B. (2014). *The body keeps the score*. New York, NY: Viking Books.

Watson, S. (2013). *Volunteering may be good for body and mind*. Boston, MA: Harvard University. Retrieved from https://www.health.harvard.edu/blog/volunteering-may-be-good-for-body-and-mind-201306266428